Rush

Hour

Rush Hour

Surprise Sithole

Rush Hour

© Copyright 2008 by Surprise Sithole

Unless otherwise indicated, all Scripture quotations are taken from the New King James Version. Copyright © 1982 by Thomas Nelson, Inc. Used by permission. All rights reserved.
Scripture quotations marked (NASB) are taken from the New American Standard Bible, © the Lockman Foundation 1960, 1962, 1963, 1968, 1971, 1972, 1973, 1975, 1977.
Scripture quotations marked (NLT) are taken from the Holy Bible, New Living Translation, copyright © 1996. Used by permission of Tyndale House Publishers, Inc., Wheaton, Illinois 60189. All rights reserved.

Published by:
MOW Books
P.O. Box 212204
Columbia, South Carolina 29221-2204
www.MountainOfWorship.com
worship@MountainOfWorship.com
(803)-665-8990

MOW Books is a ministry of Mountain Of Worship, a South Carolina non-profit organization dedicated to perpetuate the event of sustained, perpetual lifestyle worship of Jesus Christ, that releases a heavenly demonstration that causes the lost to bow their knee and the found to adore the One they live for
... until every knee bows ... until every tongue tells ... both the lost and the found ... in heaven and in hell ... that
JESUS is Lord!

ISBN 978-1-60458-183-6

Printed in the United States of America
For worldwide Distribution

Contents

Forward   ii

Preface   iii

Chapter 1:   The Joy of Obedience 1

Chapter 2:   Iris Ministries 25

Chapter 3:   Changed: Revival 101 35

Chapter 4:   The Cost of Doing Great Things 39

Chapter 5:   How to Have a Good Day 51

Chapter 6:   Visions and Dreams 59

Chapter 7:   The Rush Hour 75

Chapter 8:   The Importance of Communication 81

Chapter 9:   The Example of Peter's Life 85

Chapter 10: Whom Does God Use? 99

Chapter 11: Going Back to the Holy Land 103

Chapter 12: Abiding In Jesus 111

Forward

I first met Surprise "Supressa" Sithole when a friend asked me to take him to see a prophetic father who lived in North Carolina. I was immediately taken by the fact that there was nothing he shared that brought attention to himself. His love for Jesus poured out of every conversation. Joy filled that car during that ride and as we neared our destination, a cloud came into that car as he began giving me a prophetic word. The word was clear and precise and spoke things to me that Jesus had spoken to me in secret. I was undone and almost had to pull off the road. A few hours later we emerged from that home where that prophetic father indicated to me an anointing like had not seen. The fruit on Surprise is genuine. The joy is unforgettable. The Presence of Jesus is all over him. In many of the conferences we have done, the children, both in age and in heart, have often run up to the front to sit on the floor because there is something of Jesus on Surprise!

As I have read this book, I have been remarkably changed in my thinking. It is a book filled with visions and dreams and a reality of a world that is the realm of God, and so often not the realm of men. Initially, I thought some of the accounts were visions, but I was wrong. They were actual accounts of supernatural interventions. They were the invasion of Heaven on the life of a humble servant.

I feel so honored to have been asked to play a role in this book. I feel like I am reading Acts 29. The reality of Jesus is alive and well through the life of our precious brother.

Rush Hour is a powerful call to the Heart of Our Father and His desire for the Nations. It demands a single response... radical and single focused love and obedience to the Holy Spirit. It is a call into a place where the favor of God rests. Surprise calls us to the places of humility, destiny, and love that have been orchestrated by the Father for our lives. The wealth is not in the realms of earthly possessions... God is giving Nations to those who love His Heart! The miraculous is not the focus of this book, but this book will lead you to experience the miraculous that surrounds the One you love, because you will find yourself in His Presence often as you read through the chapters that await you.

I have found myself laughing out loud and weeping for a heart that still needs so much more of the Jesus that I read about on these pages!

May you find yourself stepping into destiny that you were created for from the foundation of the earth... the destiny that the harvest holds for you... may you be drawn into this Rush Hour of God's Purposes!

Danny Steyne
Mountain Of Worship
Columbia SC
2007

Preface

I was in an intense vision where I saw a thick cloud and I heard the sound of trumpets, thunders, and lightning, and when the Ancient of Days spoke with the voice of man, it was like rushing water.[1] He commissioned me to tell the harvesters to rush into the fields, that the fields are ripe. Then there was a response of Heavenly hosts and they said, "Now is the time". [3]

For the first three and a half years after I received Jesus I had intense visions everyday. Several of these visions are recorded in this book. The visions in this book have been selected to stir up the passion of God's heart for the lost of this world and to invite you into the ripe harvest fields.

1 Revelation 1:15

2 John 4:35

3 John 4:23

Chapter 1

The Joy of Obedience

The Voice Call

John 10:16 "I have other sheep, which are not of this fold; I must bring them also, and they will hear My voice; and they will become one flock with one shepherd."

Through Jesus, we become one in the family of Abraham. As the Bible says, we were strangers and foreigners in God's kingdom. Jesus came to destroy the wall of separation. There is no Greek or Jew in God's Kingdom; we are all one.

John 10:27 My sheep hear **My voice**, and I know them, and they follow Me.

In 1982 the Lord called me with His tender mercy. I heard a very loud voice while I was in my mother's house. We lived in a village called Sabe, in the Caixote zone of Mozambique. (Sabe means *knowledge*; Caixote means *box*). The voice said 'move from your home.' It came a second time that same night and it was much louder than the first time. It seemed to be loud enough for the entire world to hear it. The mat where I was sleeping was shaking from the sound. The voice again said 'move from your home.' That very night I obeyed the voice, got up and decided to leave.

As I went to leave, I was able to open the barred door and walk out into the African night without waking up my family. They were still asleep in the house and never heard the voice. My mistake was that I did not tell my family about the voice. I just went outside and headed to a friends house that was about two kilometers away from my house. I went to the house of a schoolmate, my friend Gafar. When I arrived at his house, I told him all about the voice I heard and that I was going to leave the village.

All I know is that I was going to a place that I did not know; I was leaving the place of *knowledge;* I was leaving the *box.* The Lord had prepared a place for me even before I was born. We started our walk that night heading to the north from Sabe and two weeks later, we reach a place called Villa Nova, which means *New Town.* That is where we met a man waiting for us. His name was Lukas. When he saw us, he immediately invited us into his home.

We were very excited because it was still early evening, in the cool of the day, and we had a place to go with no questions asked. Such a relief and difference from the last two weeks, walking through wild animal infested jungles (though none attacked us), eating wild fruits and staying protected by the trees. Although we did encounter some baboons, making lots of noise, looking at us as if they wanted to say something. It was as if they knew something we did not.

The following morning, after breakfast, Lukas called us and asked, "Where are you coming from and where are you going?" I started to tell him about the Voice that called me during the night. But Lukas, being a very wise man interrupted me by asking, "Do you know who created the Heaven and the Earth?" We said "no" and he began telling us the story of Creation. He told us that God had created us in His own image, and that God has a plan for each one of us; that every one of us could believe in Jesus and receive him into our lives. That we have to live our lives according to His will and that if we refuse, we are to go to the eternal judgment. When he said this I started crying, I felt like I had wasted my life, that I should had done this years before, but now it was too late. However, Lukas said to us "You still have time and opportunity to do this". Then he led us through a prayer of commitment to the Lord. Afterward I felt so relieved as if the entire world had changed. That morning, my friend Gafar and I gave our lives to Jesus. The joy of the Lord filled my heart from that day forward, as I had never experienced before.

A few days later, some fishermen from my village told me that my family had died, although they did not explain how it happened. I actually did not hear the whole story of how it happened until May 2005, while I was in Morrumbala, Mozambique. I was at a Healing Meeting with Todd Bentley only forty-five kilometers from the village in which I grew up. All the people from my village and the rest of my family were present at that meeting. They told me that my family had been poisoned from the bile of a crocodile, which was added to the food they all ate, by someone wanting to kill them. My mother died first, then my sister and finally my father.

From 1982, when I left my home for the last time at the Voice of the Lord, I have never set my feet back into my village. Whenever I hear that loud voice and He says go, I always obey.

> Jeremiah 7:23 But this is what I commanded them, saying, 'Obey **My voice**, and I will be your God, and you will be My people; and you will walk in all the way which I command you, that it may be well with you.'

God requires us to obey his voice and to walk in His ways. Because of our struggles in life, He has provided a way for us. The way provided is Jesus. As He said, no one can go to the Father except through Him. The Father is pleased with those who are in Jesus.

The Call of God

In Philippians, the Apostle Paul knew that there was a call on his life. Paul believed that others wanted that calling for their own lives, so therefore he pressed into his call so no one could take it from him. We each have a call on our lives that is very precious and we all need to press into the goal so that we would receive the prize.

> Philippians 3:14-16   [14] I press toward the goal for the prize of the upward **call** of God in Christ Jesus.
> [15] Therefore let us, as many as are mature, have this mind; and if in anything you think otherwise, God will reveal even this to you. [16] Nevertheless, to the degree that we have already attained, let us walk by the same rule, let us be of the same mind.

1 Corinthians 14:1 Pursue love, and desire spiritual gifts, but especially that you may prophesy.

God draws us into special gifts that He gives us for our specific call. These gifts are those that help our ministries. They help us touch people with the hand of God. The apostle Paul says we have to desire the spiritual gifts. Our lives are useless as a believer without God's gifts. Jesus told those who were with him at His ascension to stay there until they were clothed with power from on high. The power of the Holy Spirit is necessary for us to do what we are called to do. Our children and generations to come will receive these gifts as well, because His promises are ours.

Romans 11:29 For the gifts and the **calling** of God are irrevocable.

1 Thessalonians 4:7-8 For God did not **call** us to uncleanness, but in holiness. [8] Therefore he who rejects this does not reject man, but God, who has also given us His Holy Spirit.

Matthew 20:16 So the last will be first, and the first last. For many are **called**, but few chosen.

With these special gifts, there is a high calling for humility. Jesus says that the last would be first and the first will be last. Many are called but few are chosen. He is teaching us to be humble. Many of us, when we come into the Kingdom, forget the way of humility. God will always use us when we consider others better than we do ourselves. When we deem others

> **We must not think of ourselves wiser or greater than others. We have to seek a lower place.**

higher than we regard ourselves, God will consider us and call us to greater things. We must not think of ourselves wiser or greater than others. We have to seek a lower place.

Luke 16:10 If you are faithful in little things, you will be faithful in large ones. But if you are dishonest in little things, you won't be honest with greater responsibilities. (NLT)

1 Corinthians 1:26-30 [26] For you see your calling, brethren, that not many wise according to the flesh, not many mighty, not many noble, are called. [27] But God has chosen the foolish things of the world to put to shame the wise, and God has chosen the weak things of the world to put to shame the things which are mighty; [28] and the base things of the world and the things which are despised God has chosen, and the things which are not, to bring to nothing the things that are, [29] that no flesh should glory in His presence. [30] But of Him you are in Christ Jesus, who became for us wisdom from God—and righteousness and sanctification and redemption—

Isaiah 42: 6-7 [6]"I, the Lord, have called You in
  righteousness, and will hold Your hand;
  I will keep You and give You as a covenant to the
  people
  As a light to the Gentiles,
[7] To open blind eyes,
  To bring out prisoners from the prison,
  Those who sit in darkness from the prison house.

When God spoke about Jesus through the prophet Isaiah, and proclaimed that Jesus Himself is the covenant to us; and that through Him we are righteous to God. That same authority and promise given to Jesus, He gives to us, to set the captive free and to open the blind eyes. This is the calling of God to us.

> 2 Peter 1:3-7,10 ^{3} as His divine power has given to us all things that pertain to life and godliness, through the knowledge of Him who **called** us by glory and virtue, ^{4} by which have been given to us exceedingly great and precious promises, that through these you may be partakers of the divine nature, having escaped the corruption that is in the world through lust.
> ^{5}But also for this very reason, giving all diligence, add to your faith virtue, to virtue knowledge, ^{6} to knowledge self-control, to self-control perseverance, to perseverance godliness, ^{7}to godliness brotherly kindness, and to brotherly kindness love.
> ^{10} Therefore, brethren, be even more diligent to make your **call** and election sure, for if you do these things you will never stumble;
>
> 1 Peter 2:9 But you are a chosen generation, a royal priesthood, a holy nation, His own special people, that you may proclaim the praises of Him who **called** you out of darkness into His marvelous light;

Our identity in Christ is to proclaim His Word and teach people who they are in Christ and how they can grasp their destiny.

Ephesians 4:1-6 ¹ I, therefore, the prisoner of the Lord, beseech you to walk worthy of the **calling** with which you were called, ² with all lowliness and gentleness, with longsuffering, bearing with one another in love, ³ endeavoring to keep the unity of the Spirit in the bond of peace. ⁴ There is one body and one Spirit, just as you were called in one hope of your calling; ⁵ one Lord, one faith, one baptism; ⁶ one God and Father of all, who is above all, and through all, and in you all.

2 Timothy 1:8-9 ⁸Therefore do not be ashamed of the testimony of our Lord, nor of me His prisoner, but share with me in the sufferings for the gospel according to the power of God, ⁹ who has saved us and called us with a holy calling, not according to our works, but according to His own purpose and grace which was given to us in Christ Jesus before time began,

Hebrews 3:1 Therefore, holy brethren, partakers of the heavenly calling, consider the Apostle and High Priest of our confession, Christ Jesus,

Acts 2:39 For the promise is to you and to your children, and to all who are afar off, as many as the Lord our God will call."

My Childhood

My parents had five girls after their firstborn, my brother. They expected another girl, but they were going to "try" and have a boy. They actually planned on naming me 'Try.' When I was born, there was a portion of my hair on the right side that was white so they said that it was a surprise; a baby born with white hair. That is why they named me Surprise.

When I was 6 months old, I crawled over to the dog's food and began to eat with him. However, the dog did not know that I was a child and thought that I was coming to finish his food, so he bit me. The dog sunk his teeth in between my eyes and bit my right eye as well. My eyeball came out of the socket, and fell onto the floor. My family rushed to me to try and put my eye back in its place. The enemy was trying to stop my future. There was no doctor in the village, so they put a bandage on my eyes and two weeks later, I was fine, although I still have the scar on my face. It is an ongoing sign of God's protection to me.

During my childhood, I was actually not a happy child and I cried all the time. I had nightmares, saw unusual things at night, and demons tormented me. Often times at night, I would see people walking around the house. Sometimes I could even hear people cutting trees. I would see a mountain before me when there was no mountain there. These and many other scary things were a regular part of my life.

Occasionally at night when I was asleep on the mat, I felt lifted up from the mat. I could feel people lifting me off the mat. When I tried to shout for help, my voice could not come out. When I tried to help myself with my arms, my body would be stuck; I couldn't move. I would cry inside my heart and try to move on the inside but couldn't express it on the outside. After I woke up, I was in such fear that it might happen again, I couldn't get back to sleep. When I told my parents, they took me, covered me with a blanket, and started beating the drums. They said they were giving me treatment. The drums might go on all night. By midnight, they would beat me with horsehair tail and when I would feel the pain, I would cry out. When I cried out and tried to talk, they would beat the drums louder and they themselves got louder so they couldn't understand what I was saying. The interpreters would start interpreting things that I was not saying. It was such a terrible life as a child.

I always thank God that He personally came and talked to me and I received His invitation to be in His family. From that time, everything has changed and He replaced all my sorrow with joy.

It was at the border town called Villa Nova, meaning *New Town*, between Mozambique and Malawi, that I gave my life to Jesus. This is where a new beginning started for me. My old life was gone and the new life began.

The Lord took me on a journey of visions. From the day I gave my life to Jesus, I received visions and visitations every day and night. I saw Heaven opening up and people flying into it. Sometimes I would see Heavenly beings filling all the earth and other times I would see a city with all kinds of birds and they would all speak the language of man. This went on for three and a half years. It came to the point where I was feeling as if I was not a normal person. In those days, I would see everything that was going to happen the next day. Some people said that it was the beginning of a mental disorder. At that time I could not find anyone that could explain to me what was happening, but I thank God that now I know what was happening. I know it through the revelation of the Holy Spirit.

In Malawi

Gafar and I stayed with Mr. Lukas for two weeks and then we left for Malawi. We arrived in a town called Nshalo, by the Sucoma Sugar Factory, where we met a man named Silver and he welcomed us into his house. He took us to the island of Chikuseis and I began sharing my visions and experiences that I had received from the Lord with the people. I had already received the language of Chichewa from the Lord, so communication was easy.

The first day about eight people came to the Lord and that was the beginning of my new life. We stayed on that island all year and then after the first year Gafar went back to Mozambique. I handed over the new believers to the surrounding churches, but I stayed there for one more year and started a small business of buying and selling fish. I started traveling from one market to another, selling fish and preaching the Gospel. However, I did not know the Bible then and I would just tell the people of the heavenly visions and experiences I had, and the people would believe and give their lives to the Lord.

Something was bothering my life. I was new in the Lord and I didn't know about deliverance. I would dream about my family, who had died and the following day I would get into trouble, something horrible would happen to me. One day I dreamed I was having a nice time with my mother and father, the following day something bad happened. I was walking in the town of Nshalo, and I saw a group of people coming toward me, as I walked past them I saw that they were beating a thief. I heard the thief say, "Oh, that man sold me the stuff" (pointing to me). I was simply walking along unaware of what was going on, when all of a sudden they began to beat me with out reason. They didn't allow me to talk they just took us both to the police. When we arrived at the station, I noticed the police officer in charge was a friend of mine (a fellow believer who knew my story) and he tried to find out the true story. What he found out was that my statement was right, that I was an innocent bystander. I was just passing by. So they released me, with my face still swollen. I walked out from the police station while the other man remained in prison. This continued to happen. Whenever I had a dream, bad things would happen the next day until eventually I went through deliverance.

One morning, while still in Malawi, I went to Tengani Village at the area called Nshenga to the Shire Shore to buy some fresh fish. The fishermen commonly fish all night so in the morning they return to sell the catch and I was there waiting for them that morning. There were not many buyers around. As a result, I was able to get a good price on many fish. So many, that they had to help me carry them back to the compound where I was staying. When I got all the fish back, I realized I did not have enough wood to dry up the stock so I went to my neighbor to borrow an axe. He gave me one so I went in to the bush to cut some wood and while I was cutting; I heard a noise like heh, heh, heh. I couldn't identify the noise so I went to find the animal thinking that I might be able to kill and sell it. As I was going to hunt the animal, the noise was getting quieter, so I continued to pursue it. I came very close to the animal not knowing what it was. It was a python, and she was ready for attack. My right foot stepped on her and she tried to wrap around and squeeze my foot while her tail was waving around trying to catch me. I thank God that I was shorter at that time and that her tail swung over my head and my feet were outside of her trap; her circle of death. I saw the tail just passing above my head circling and it was making so much noise as it hit the grass, it sounded like a loud wind. The snake was fighting with the bushes thinking that I was caught in them because of the high grass. Fear struck me. I threw away the ax and ran away with my trousers all wet, unaware of where I was going. For two weeks, I was in such fear that I did not sleep well.

Isaiah 54:17 No weapon formed against you shall prosper, and every tongue which rises against you in judgment you shall condemn. This is the heritage of the servants of the LORD, and their righteousness is from Me," Says the LORD.

As the Bible says, "no weapon formed against you shall prosper...this is our heritage". The heritage of the servants of the Lord is to overcome. I thank God for rescuing me out of the mouth of the python. I believe that he likes to rescue everyone that cries for help, my encouragement to you is to ask for help from the Lord, He will help you. He will lift you up when you are in trouble. If you are sad, He will comfort you with His Spirit.

The last year that I was in Malawi, it was during a time of war in Mozambique. The war had reached a point that people in most of the surrounding provinces had to flee to Malawi. Most of the people gathered in the south at a place called Ntowe. When I heard that the people from Mozambique were going to the south I decided to go there because I thought it would be a good opportunity for me to sell my fish to them.

I left Malawi and went to Ntowe, to begin doing business of buying and selling fish. While I was selling my fish, I also evangelized the people. Many came to the Lord. Many of those were young people that formed a group that would meet everyday and then go out to different markets preaching the word. The group was very strong in unity. Every Sunday we would go and visit different churches and the Lord was with us.

> Revelation 3:20 Behold, I stand at the door and knock. If anyone hears my voice and opens the door, I will come in to him and dine with him, and he with me.

The Land Mine

I left Malawi going back to my country, Mozambique where there was a war and all the roads were blocked. There were only two days a week where we could travel. All the cars would gather in one area and on those two days, the soldiers would accompany us to the next location. No one traveled alone. Soldiers accompanied everyone. I took a bus to the border in Mwanza, Malawi and then I walked to the Mozambique border in Zobwe to the next soldier escort location. When I arrived, the people told me there was no transportation going that day.

The following day, by 5:00 am there was a noise of whistles and singing. I said to those sleeping with me, "Who are those people singing in the distance?" They said that they are the Frelimo Soldiers coming to escort us today. We were going to Tete, and I said to my friend whom I had just met at the border that I needed to go to Beira another five hundred kilometers (over three hundred miles) south of Tete. He also told me I needed to get another escort that would take me from Tete to Beira through Zimbabwe because all other roads were blocked and it was the only way open for travel because the straight road to Beira was blocked my Renamo soldiers.

While we were speaking, the commander told us we needed to get into the trucks. There were twenty military trucks full of soldiers and guns and many civilian trucks full of passengers and goods going to all different locations in Southern Africa. Zimbabwean soldiers were escorting all these trucks from the Malawi border to the border of Zimbabwe. They started lining up the trucks and the lead truck (an ugly truck) was called Rebenta Mina, which means 'blow the land mine'. I was in truck behind this one.

As we started going the soldiers were singing and dancing in their trucks and the people were silent in theirs. As the journey went on, about forty-five kilometers from the border of Zobwe, the truck that I was in drove over a land mine and the land mine was so powerful that the truck was lifted into the air, flew like a bird and then thrown off the road. While it was flying through the air, I saw a hand, as if it were a man's hand, taking me out of the truck and putting me right in the middle of the road. The next truck in the line came quickly towards me but stopped just before getting to me. No one else from my truck survived the land mine. The soldiers stopped the entire escorted caravan of about twenty kilometers long and forced everyone to get out and lay on the ground.

After a while, we got back in. I was placed in the first truck again now with all the dead bodies and a few other people. Some soldiers came up to the truck and said there are too many people in it, and took some young men and myself out. We got into the next truck. After driving, just a short distance the truck in front of ours hit another land mine and everyone died. They then took all the dead bodies to another truck and from there we drove safely to a little town called Moatize. This is where the commander had everyone clean up. While at the refugee camp, we buried all the people that died that day. We stayed there for the evening and continued our journey to Zimbabwe two days later.

I remained in Tete for about six months during which time I really experienced the power of God. I saw first hand how incredible and beyond understanding was His grace and love. While I was in Tete, He instantly gave me the language of Nhungue. I started ministering to the people and many came to the Lord. I saw many salvations and healings in even greater numbers than when I was in Malawi. Miracles were happening openly everyday. My faith grew to a higher level and I started experiencing God's existence openly. I was circling three towns, Tete, Matundo and Moatize. The word of God spread throughout these cities and the people were encouraged. Even today, the same power that was in Jesus, that raised Him from the dead, is in us, it is in you, if you open your heart and receive it; it will manifest in you. The Lord can use you in greater ways. His desire is that all would be willing.

After a while, I decided to move on into the next phase of my destiny, which was going to Beira. I asked the Lord, and He provided for me. He provided a plane ticket from Tete to Beira (my first experience flying). Before I got onto the plane, I kneeled down in the airport terminal waiting to board the airplane. I prayed and confessed my sins and gave thanks to God. Some of the people were laughing at me thinking I was crazy and then while on the plane, I started praying again. I thought I was very close to God because I was in the sky (closer to Heaven), but the people told me if I wanted to pray I needed to pray quieter. Forty-five minutes later, I was in Beira walking in the next part of my destiny.

In Beira

Beira is a city in the central east part of Mozambique, along the Indian Ocean. I came to Beira after my adventure in Malawi and Tete on the journey of my life. When I arrived in Beira, I continued my studies and became a public nurse at Dondo Hospital. I was staying in Mafarinha and sometimes when the war was very intense in Mafarinha, I would stay at the house of Pastor Noah, who lived only eight hundred meters (about a half a mile) from the Hospital of Dondo.

One night we were having worship practice in Mafarinha unaware that the rebels were coming. Six of us young people slept together in the house after the practice. I was in a deep sleep dreaming about a beast coming to attack us and then when I opened my eyes I found that the whole house was on fire. It was a mud hut with grass roof, so I thought that it was only the house on fire but the whole village was actually on fire. I woke up and started to tell my friends what was going on but before I could explain, the roof began falling in on us. We were planning to go out the door but there were rebels all over the village so instead we dug a hole in the wall. I thank God that it was a mud hut, because if it had been concrete we would not have been able to get out and this testimony of His provision would not exist. After we dug the hole in the wall I was the first to exit, but I could not see anything because of all the smoke. I was just running all around and I could not see the others. After a few minutes, my eyes adjusted and I was able to see and run to a safe place. I went to the Dondo train station and my friends went to the church where they stayed until the next morning. The next day I was back at the hospital again helping with all the injured people from the previous night's battle. It was a mass of confusion, death and blood at the hospital.

In June 1989, the medical doctors and nurses were on strike, so I left my job to pursue God and His Voice. I got a ticket on the boat to Buzi, which is west of Beira. In those days, you could only go to Buzi by boat. We left in the morning, but after only two hours, we had to stop. It was low tide and we were stuck on the sand. There were many police on the boat at 10:00 am on transfer to Buzi. While everyone was waiting for the tide to change, just standing around bored, I stood and began preaching the Gospel. Many people including some of the police officers gave their lives to Jesus Christ that day. I think the boat stopped on the sand for a reason that day. I had gone to Buzi without any plan, without preparation, but knowing inside of me that there was a calling for God to do something in Buzi. By 2:00 pm, the tide started coming in and we began our journey again towards Buzi. The police called me 'the priest'.

That day I met the Mayor of Buzi at his house. He was also a believer, from the Assemblies of God church. I stayed there for three weeks preaching the Gospel to the students from Banda Secondary School. The students were camping in military tents because the rebels had destroyed their school. The Lord gave me so much favor to preach to them. Those students were on fire for the Lord. We had many outreaches with the students going to all the surrounding areas. That developed a very strong team at the school. I would also go visit the police who had given their lives to Jesus on the boat and I would share the word of God, they respected me so much because of my boldness on the boat. We saw many healings and salvations at this time in the town of Buzi as well. At each house where we went, the people would say they knew something was going to happen; they that someone was coming with some news they had not heard before. That made it much easier for them to receive what we were saying because they already had a dream of it. Wherever we went, the people were open and ready to receive. Again, I saw the working miracle of God.

This incredibly successful trip was completely 'unstrategized,' just as the Bible says, "everything works out for good to those who love God and are called according to His purposes." (Romans 8:28) When I saw that my mission was over, I decided to go back Beira. However, I didn't leave all those new converts unattended; I introduced them to the Assemblies of God church and other churches in Buzi that preach salvation and obedience to the Holy Spirit so that they would continue to grow in the Lord. In December 1989, I decided to go to South Africa.

In South Africa

I arrived in South Africa on January 3, 1990 and stayed on the farm of a man named Jim Teckleyberg. He provided for me to go to Bible School in Durban and when I arrived there, I found out that it was an English speaking school and they did not accept Portuguese-speaking people. I had an interview with Pastor Fun Sabise. Spontaneously, I began talking to this man in a tongue I didn't know, not knowing what I was saying. I was speaking in English. That is how the gift of English came. He said to me "you speak very good English, where did you learn the language?" At that time, I did not know if I gave him the right answer or not. The man said to me, 'you are admitted to this Bible School.'

I enjoyed life at the Bible School. The Lord also gave me the language Zulu and I was helped translate at the school. I was able to help the school doing translation from English to Zulu and vice versa. For the next three years, we went on several outreaches and visited different mission organizations. In the beginning of 1994, after finishing Bible School in South Africa I came to a town called Malelane. When I arrived there, I did not find a place to live so I started living in the bush on the mountains around Malelane. During the day, I would preach at the schools, communities and farms.

One day I met a couple and their three children. They were all living together in Baulosi near Capumeden and they invited me to come and stay with them. I shared a room with their son even though it was very difficult time in South Africa because of the old apartheid regime. Gart and Annalee Nell suffered much rejection from their family, because the family would not visit them as a result of my staying with them. In those days, it was rare to find a native African living with an Afrikaans family. Their faith was so strong and they loved me so much more than my natural family that I stayed with them and had a wonderful time during 1994 and half of 1995.

I felt so close to God when I was with this family. They were such an awesome family. We prayed together every morning from 4:00-5:00 am, and it was during this time that we started a Bible School in Malelane called Harvest Action. We had students from all over South Africa learning in the Bible School and we used material from the Timothy Training Institute. When the mission was over in Malelane, other people took over the Bible School and The Nell's went to Durban. I stayed in Malelane for a while and then decided to move on. It was in Malelane where I saw people with mental illness healed and many salvations. This is where I met Heidi Baker.

White River

While I was living in Malelane, I felt that the Lord was calling me out of this place, and so I started praying, asking Him for direction. I had a vision. *I was fishing in one of the rivers and as I was fishing, I was struggling and not catching any fish. A woman came to me and said, take your hooks, go to the white river, and start to fish there.* Later I asked the Lord for the meaning of the vision. He gave me no answer because the Lord knows about time, and He knew that He was preparing a suitable time for me. I then received three prophetic words and all of them were saying that my job in Malelane was over. On November 10, 1995, I had the same vision again. The following day, on the 11th, a woman named Annalee called me from Durban. She told me that the Lord was saying it was time for me to move from Malelane to White River.

I did not know anyone in White River and at the time, I did not even know that there was a place called White River. I just thought it was a river with clear water. However, when she called, she told me there was a place called White River and the Lord told her I was to move there. So, on November 15 I left for White River.

When I arrived there, I asked the Lord who to approach to ask for a place to live, and He led me to a farm that had just been bought the previous month by John and Antoinette Robinson. They gave me a house to live in on the farm and immediately I began preaching.

The first day I went to the Platsak farm and started preaching. Four women and three men gave their lives to Jesus and afterward I talked to the owner of the farm, Danny

VanStaden, to see if he would provide a place for us to fellowship. He gave us a storeroom to meet in. We cleaned it up and started having fellowship together.

During this time, another pastor, William Wid, invited me to translate his material. I translated it into Zulu and Portuguese. Pastor William and I would also go preaching together into all the bus stations around Mpumalanga province. The region was very touched. There were many miracles and lots of salvations and churches were planted all over the province and even into other provinces. Miracles accompanied the ministry. I stayed on the farm for ten years and we became family with the owners of the farm. While on the farm, I got married to Tryphina and we had our three boys.

How I met my Wife

In 1993, when I was twenty-five years old, I started praying and asking God for my wife. In 1994, I saw my first vision of my future wife. As I was praying, I saw a chalkboard coming toward me with two colors, pink and blue. I asked the Lord for the explanation, but at the time, He did not give me one. Then again, at the end of 1994, I had the same vision a second time. Again, I inquired from the Lord for the explanation and again I did not get a response.

So one Tuesday morning I went to prayer and fasting. I was part of a group of about eight people that would meet for prayer every Tuesday from 8:00 am to 12:00 pm. Each time we would write prayer requests, put them on the table and then we would all pray over them. So this particular day my request said "Lord please give me a Wife." When Gart saw my request he said to me, we will not pray for this today but something else that is more important. I said to him that this was very important to me and then Gart said, "When you find a woman and her name is Tryphina, she is yours." At the time, I did not believe him I thought he was just joking.

In May 1995, while I was still in Malelane, we started outreach from South Africa to Zimbabwe and Chimoio, Nhaminga and Beira all in Mozambique. After crossing the Border Control in Messina, driving to Masvingo, the vision of pink and blue came to me a third time, while I was in a truck with five other people. I started praying asking God about the vision. As I was doing this, the pastor seated on my left side asked me "When are you going to get married?" I said to him, "How could I marry without knowing the one to marry?" At that time, I was 27 years old. He said to me, "You have to get married because you are getting old". As he was saying those words, I had a vision. I said to myself, "Whenever I see the woman wearing the colors *pink on top and blue on the bottom* that will be my wife." That was the sign, so in Zimbabwe I had a good time looking, but I did not find anyone in Chimoio or Nhaminga and finally in Beira, where we spent three days.

Then, Thursday around 4:00 to 5:00 pm, I was visiting my cousin, the daughter of my sister, when suddenly I saw a young woman wearing *pink on top and blue on the bottom*, coming from school. My heart started pumping fast within me. I called for her to come closer and she came. My first words to her were, "I need you to be my secretary, to write my history". She said to give her the books and she would do it for me. Then I said to her "Not only that, but a longer life together." She laughed and walked away.

The following day, at the same time, I went to the same place and she was coming home from school again. I asked my cousin to talk to her nicely for me, and she did, so she came again to me. I asked her name and she said Tryphina. Then I believed Garts' prophecy and the vision that I had received. When I realized that all was fulfilled I started resting in God's purpose for me in marriage, and pursuing the process of a relationship with Tryphina. In 1996, we were married.

She became a great help to the ministry. We traveled to many places planting churches in the cities and countryside. She was first a mother to the many children we took in, because we always had four or five children in the house before we had any of our own. We now have three boys, the first is Enoch, and the second is Love and the third Israel. Tryphina is a worshipper and a teacher of worship and flows in the gift of prophecy. Supernaturally the Lord started pouring the gift of languages into her.

I have learned something about waiting on God. If I was not a person who waits on God, I could have married the wrong wife. Now I can say that I have a good wife because the Lord gave her to me. In 1994, the Lord did not want to explain the vision. He needed me to have the explanation in the right time. I continued praying for that God would bring me a wife, although when I received the vision I didn't know who it was that He would bring into my life; I had no idea what was in my hands. I believe there are many people out there who already have something from God, although they do not know what it is. We have to ask God to open our eyes.

Three things that I have learned through this process: first is to ask, second is persevere and wait on God and the third is to receive with all faith.

Chapter 2

Iris Ministries

I met Heidi Baker in 1995 when she came to our meeting. Johannes Schonken was the pastor in Malelane, South Africa, at that time. I attended the service that day. After the service, I talked with Heidi and she gave me her business card. Twice, in visions, in 1996 I saw her standing in Mozambique calling out to me. I decided to pursue the vision and look for her. I sought out Johannes but he was not to be found. After that I went to another mutual friend, James, and he told me to go to the house of another pastor, Mashava, and he could tell me where Johannes could be found.

When I arrived on a Pastor Mashava's home, on February 24, 1997, he was in Chimoio but his wife and children were at home. The children took me to Boa Nova where there was a tent, one camper and a church. That night as I was sleeping in the camper with Matthew, a young man from England, I fell three times from the chair because I kept hearing the phone ringing. The first time I thought I was going to answer the call. Matthew woke up when I went to answer the phone and asked me what I was doing. I told him I heard the phone ringing and was answering the phone. He said, "Surprise, there is no phone!" The second time the same thing happened. Finally, the third time I realized that it was the call of God to that ministry. I thanked God Almighty for the events of that night.

The following day I went to Heidi Baker's house, where I met a man from Seattle named Gordon Haggerty. I believe we met by divine appointment. It was as if we met a long time ago. We started praying that day for hours, crying before the Lord. Later that afternoon, I met Heidi. It was as if we had been working together for a long time. That was on February 25, 1997. From that time forward the Lord made Himself evident with many wonders. I am an eyewitness of everything that has been happening up to this very day.

Iris Ministries had recently lost all their buildings at Chihango, and so this was a very difficult period of time for them. I began serving the Lord at Iris Ministries in the center of Machava. We were all living in tents most of which were military tents and one very large one.

A vision of Heaven

On a Thursday, in June 1997, the Lord took me to Heaven. I was having a strange feeling that day. I knew that I was about to see something but I did not know what was about to happen. I was tired as if I wanted to sleep but there was no sleep on me at that time. I went to my room to pray and as I was praying, I heard a noise that I could not describe. It was as if the wind was taking me somewhere and I suddenly saw myself going higher into the heavens.

When I arrived there, I saw many Acacia trees. All the trees were in a line and had appeared to have been pruned the day before. As I walked on the streets of pure gold, going from west to east, I saw the rising sun; however, it was not a natural sun; there was something glorious rising, a very thick glory. All the trees were in order, lined up from east to west and from north to south. As I walked, I looked on the sides of the street and there were clusters of leftover gold on the ground.

On my left, a cloud was talking to me, and this cloud was more intelligent than I was. He was giving me answers to the thoughts of my heart; explaining to me the things that I was thinking in the deep parts of my mind. As I was looking at this leftover gold, immediately the cloud said, "Look at this gold, we throw it on earth and the kings of the earth fight for the leftovers, because they do not know the real wealth is here in Heaven."

I was thinking of how I was going to greet God, because I knew I was going to face him. How could I offer acceptable honor and respect to Him? The cloud told me, "God doesn't need all you think he needs, He just needs your obedience." I began thinking several things. "Where are the Jews?" I did not know. I started thinking "Have I been raptured up to Heaven?" While I was thinking this, the cloud spoke to me, "Son, forget that. Wait for the time; right now look down on Earth." Immediately, I remembered that I left Earth so I looked down following his direction, and saw two brothers standing on the Earth: there was an older brother with a younger brother. I said to the cloud, "I see two brothers standing there on earth." Then the cloud said to me "I am giving you a mission, go and tell them to get their lives in order and give their lives to the Savior while it is day before the night will come and it will be difficult for them to do so. Heaven is not a place to fix your life but a place to enjoy."

Then I felt like I was falling from the 101st floor all the way down to the ground and I arrived back here on earth.

While the vision continued, I saw the brothers still standing in the same place I had seen them from Heaven. I began preaching to them as if I were a dying man. The younger brother took the Savior into his heart with gladness and repentance and while he was repenting, the cloud came to where I was standing. The cloud asked me, "What do you see?" I said to the cloud, "I am seeing the repentance of the younger brother." As the younger brother repented, the favor of the Father was on him; he was clothed in white and moved with the authority of the Father. However, the older brother was jealous of the younger brother. The cloud said to me, what you see is right. The older brother is a representation of all the Jews and the younger of all the Gentiles. The favor of the Lord is going to be poured out so much more on the younger brother. There is coming a time when the Jews will be jealous of the Christians, because they know that they were first called to the Kingdom. Now they are becoming last to receive the glory of God. The Gentiles, even though called last, are now becoming first in the favor of the Lord.

The Friday after the vision, we organized an all-night prayer meeting in the tent of Mama Aida (Heidi's African name). We gathered all the children and we started praying. As we prayed that evening, there were sparkles of fire in the tent all through the meeting. The Lord began pouring open visions on small children. All the small children, that were there, saw visions -- some of them were taken to Heaven -- some saw angels. That night, in 1997, God came into the tent and it was there that we saw the reality of the Living God. Some of the children, Tomajito and Edgas, who had seen visions, now live at Iris base in Pemba. It was amazing to watch God reveal His mysteries to His little babies. If you want a greater revelation of the mystery of God, first you need to become as a little child.

Some of the events that happen in Iris Ministries are extremely amazing. Here is an excerpt from Rolland Baker's writings.

3 AUGUST, MAPUTO, MOZAMBIQUE -- Surpresa Sithole, our Mozambican national director, seems incapable of a negative thought. Brimming over with the Holy Spirit, he grins broadly and laughs easily in all circumstances. He is my constant companion in the bush, and we go everywhere preaching together. Jesus supernaturally called him away from his village witch doctor parents and made him a powerful leader among our churches.

Beside me in our heavily loaded Cessna 206 is Surpresa Sithole, our international director of Iris Ministries along with Heidi and me. He incessantly presses me in the Lord for more ministry flights to the north and west of Africa, and beyond. Darfur, Ethiopia, Angola, and on to the Middle East -- our vision is revival, visitation and the unmeasured outpouring of the Holy Spirit all the way to Jerusalem from southern Africa. The seeds of this movement sprang up in 1998 with a small band of pastors who gathered for Bible school at our fledgling children's center in Maputo, Mozambique. Since then a fiery hunger for God has spread across the land in spite of floods, famines, weaknesses and troubles without number, heavy demonic attack, and the world's worst poverty.

The little town of Bangula appears, and then the dirt runway. It looks great after we had it cleared of tall weeds last week. No one has landed here since I last flew in almost two years ago. We touch down in the hazy twilight and send up a huge cloud of blowing dust. Off in the grass I shut down and immediately hundreds of children come running toward us. Our missionary Pam Bryan appears with a truck and the pastor's press in also, laughing and excitedly hugging Steve, Gordon, Surpresa and me as we climb out of our plane. Somehow, in the dark we unload our gear and sound equipment with lots of shouting and jumping all around. This is such a major event.

We get to Pam's rented house just by the runway. It is old, plain and bare, and in need of much repair. You brush your teeth under a faucet in the dirt courtyard and take cold bucket baths. There is a squat toilet in the back. However, it is a real brick house, not a mud hut, and it is wonderful by local standards. (from Rolland & Heidi Baker's Newsletter, August 2002)

BANGULA, MALAWI -- The full moon is bright, casting sharp shadows from the thick trees overhead. The warm night air is loud with the cries of hundreds of voices. In the dirt alongside the road, without lights or sound equipment, village pastors are on their faces calling out to Jesus, "Be with us! Stay with us! Never leave us! We have to have you! We want you! We love you!" They are shaking. They are crying. Their wives are there too, tears running down their faces. Even their little children, barefoot and in rags, are bowing down, praying with faces in their hands. Surpresa and I move around in the dark, praying for everyone we can. "Love them, Jesus! Love them intensely tonight! Be with them! Show yourself to them!" Some fall to the ground and just stay there, reveling in His touch and company.

They are not alone. Jesus is with them. Nothing will separate them from His love. I just flew from Mozambique in my Cessna, and many of them have walked for days to meet with me here near a small town in Malawi centered among many of our destitute country churches. They are in crisis. The Gospel is being tested. Malawi's worst famine in fifty years has been descending on this area for months. Floods and then drought have destroyed crop after crop. Malawi is already one of the world's ten poorest countries, often in serious trouble, but now the government has announced that seventy percent of its people are at risk of starvation.

Our pace continues to accelerate. In May, we hosted hundreds of visitors who came to participate in major conferences in the bush of Mozambique and Malawi, a tremendous logistical challenge. Thirty thousand gathered in the remote town of Morrumbala, Surpresa's birthplace, for meetings with Todd Bentley and his Fresh Fire team, and twenty thousand in Bangula, Malawi, with Che Ahn and his HIM team. We and our staff threw ourselves into the ministry with all our hearts and strength as well, seeing God do many miracles among us all. We have so much more to report!

Next, our staff journeyed to Bilene far to the south for our annual staff retreat, a richly appreciated and needed time when our own Iris family could relax and enjoy the powerful presence of God. Heidi, Surpresa and I loved this chance to bless and encourage our "troops," and by our prophetic guest speaker, Jill Austin.

And so the Holy Spirit is moving among us and other ministries around the world faster than we ever imagined. We have lost our love of this world. The Kingdom is our pearl of great price. Our King is our greatest possession. The poor and desperate of the world are running to Him. They will not miss His fire and glory. They will not be left behind. They will not lose the riches of their inheritance in Him.

Jesus is worth something. He is worth everything. We ask our readers, who will lose their life for Him in order to gain it? Who will suffer hardship as a good soldier of Jesus Christ, and run the race to win? Who will join us in the harvest field, sparing nothing? Who wants to burn with life and passion in pursuit of what is pure, perfect and eternal? Who wants to love as Jesus loves? (from Rolland & Heidi Baker's Newsletter, March 2002)

Our Revival in Southern Africa

The place of Revival - Floods in Mozambique along with famine and drought in Malawi:

In the Year 2000 in Southern Africa, we had an extreme amount of rainfall that led to the flooding of the land. Zambezi, Comate and Limpopo Rivers were flooded and helicopters took all of the survivors to accommodation centers in the mainland. Some of the women gave birth to their babies in trees and this is part of the history even to this day.

The women were giving birth in trees, and God was giving birth to Revival!

The people came to accommodation centers in the mainland and they gathered in schools, community halls, churches and some even in tents provided by the UN. Many there met Jesus as their savior. The WFP (World Food Program), UN, USA Air Save and South African Air Save helicopters were there every day. They were leaving early in morning with our pastors including myself (it was my first opportunity to fly in a helicopter) to go and give the food to the people and search for more survivors. When we arrived, the people said to us, "Please give us the word of God first and then the food because we are sinners we need a savior to save our souls, now is the time." This is when we had a great opportunity of sharing the word to all the survivors in the camps. People were coming to the Lord in large numbers, even the government officials. With one voice they said, "Please feed us with the word." We fed them all with the Word of God and with natural food.

Many of those events that happened were recorded in newspapers and magazines. Revival broke out over the entire land and into other countries in southern Africa. The revival brought more hunger for God and more passion for Jesus. The people were going village to village, walking for days and hours to reach other people. Wherever there was a church of fifty people because of revival, it would lead to fifty churches. Almost every member knew how to plant a church and how to reach a neighbor. I believe revival is when a great hunger comes and when the people have this hunger they are filled with God's great power as it says in Matthew 5:6, "Blessed are those who hunger and thirst for righteousness because they will be filled." Through our revival in southern Africa, the people were filled with God's righteousness and we saw so much healing. More than had been seen in the previous five hundred years since Christianity was introduced in the land. New songs were written and the people worshipped God with great passion and intimacy. The gifts flowed to almost every believer who had hunger for it. To this day revival continues. Our prayer is that the Lord would keep the revival burning; we do not want this revival to stop. We have a goal, to see this revival going all the way to Jerusalem and to see that all nations receive the same passion and revival fill the whole world. Our prayer is that revival will remain until Jesus comes to fetch his bride. As He says, *"I am with you always, even to the end of the age." Matthew 28:20b (NLT)*

Chapter 3

Changed: Revival 101

Helping a New Convert in Revival

A move of God had begun and now it was sweeping the nations of the earth. Every continent was being affected. How were we going to bring people to the Lord and equip them so they could be used in this great revival?

When a new Christian comes to the Lord, we help them with the basics of following Jesus. We give them the assurance of salvation, because after initially being saved, many start to doubt their salvation and fall away in different ways. Most of them have the same question like; "How do I know for sure that I am a child of God?" Perhaps this question can be answered in one word, "Changed". When the Holy Spirit brings us to Christ, important new changes take place in our life

> 2 Corinthians 5:17 Therefore, if anyone is in Christ, he is a new creation; old things have passed away; behold, all things have become new.

We start with the basics. They must know that they have had a sinful life. And they must know of God's great love. We give them assurance of being born again, and we teach them how to walk in this new life they now have.

The five steps:

1. Be aware of our sin

1John 1:8-9 [8]If we say that we have no sin, we deceive ourselves, and the truth is not in us. [9]If we confess our sins, He is faithful and just to forgive us our sins and to cleanse us from all unrighteousness.

2. Be obedient to God

1John 2:3-5 [3]Now by this we know that we know Him, if we keep His commandments. [4]He who says, "I know Him," and does not keep His commandments, is a liar, and the truth is not in him. [5]But whoever keeps His word, truly the love of God is perfected in him. By this we know that we are in Him.

3. Receive freedom from a lifestyle of sin

1John 3:9 Whoever has been born of God does not sin, for His seed remains in him; and he cannot sin, because he has been born of God.
1John 5:18 We know that whoever is born of God does not sin; but he who has been born of God keeps himself, and the wicked one does not touch him.

4. *Learn to love others*

> 1John 3:14 We know that we have passed from death to life, because we love the brethren. He who does not love his brother abides in death.
> 1John 4:7-8 [7]Beloved, let us love one another, for love is of God; and everyone who loves is born of God and knows God. [8]He who does not love does not know God, for God is love.

5. *Believe in Jesus*

> 1John 5:1 Whoever believes that Jesus is the Christ is born of God, and everyone who loves Him who begot also loves him who is begotten of Him.
> John 1:12 But as many as received Him, to them He gave the right to become children of God, to those who believe in His name:

Throughout history, God has given every individual a chance to accept his eternal plan of salvation. Sadly, most people have rejected it. Accepting Jesus Christ as our personal Savior is the most significant decision we could ever make during our lifetime, because we will spend eternity with the Lord Jesus Christ. This is the reason of life – this is how we live with eternal results.

The enemy knows about our new life in Jesus Christ and he will fight so that we will lose the power of it, but we must ask Jesus to give us the Holy Spirit so that He can help us remain in him and continue growing. It is a great privilege to enter into God's big family here on Earth; having a taste of Heaven enjoying His Kingdom.

1 Peter 2:9 But you are a chosen generation, a royal priesthood, a holy nation, His own special people, that you may proclaim the praises of Him who called you out of darkness into His marvelous light;

Many people think that they are a Christian because of their church affiliation, their parental connection with a church, or the performance of some ritual, such as water baptism or Holy Communion. This is false assurance. The Bible makes it clear that salvation happens when the Holy Spirit takes control of our lives.

We need to continue to learn about our salvation and deepen our relationship with Jesus Christ. Because we have this new birth through faith in Christ, we must continue to ask him to forgive our sins, so that we can continue to rejoice in knowing that we are truly God's children. When we became a Christian, our whole life changed, including our emotions. New feelings replace old feelings, and we have Love, Peace and Joy.

Chapter 4

The Cost of Doing Great Things

John 5:20-21 [20] For the Father loves the Son, and shows Him all things that He Himself is doing; and the Father will show Him greater works than these, so that you will marvel. [21]For just as the Father raises the dead and gives them life, even so the Son also gives life to whom He wishes. (NASB)

God raises the dead. That is why Jesus raises the dead. Because Jesus rose from the dead, we also have to raise the dead. This is one of his commands to us when he said go preach the good news, heal the sick, cleanse the lepers and raise the dead. Freely you have received and freely you have to give.

John 14:12 "Truly, truly, I say to you, he who believes in Me, the works that I do, he will do also; and greater works than these he will do; because I go to the Father." (NASB)

We have been called for a greater work and it is right in front of us whether we see it or not. God will remain faithful to us. His desire is for us to move into our calling. The call is for the 'greater things' that Jesus promised to us.

The point is for us to believe in him as the first begotten Son of God, as the light of the world and as the true Messiah, that through him we become heirs in God's Kingdom, the princes and princesses in our Fathers house.

> Acts 2:39 "For the promise is for you and your children and for all who are far off, as many as the Lord our God will call to Himself." (NASB)

The promise of the release of the Holy Spirit through our lives will remain unfulfilled to us if we are walking outside of our calling. First, for us to receive the fullness of this promise, we need to receive the Holy Spirit. He is the key to a supernatural life and comes with all the spiritual gifts and fruits. Therefore, these gifts and fruits are for us and our children and generations to come, to all those that will receive him.

The call for the supernatural

Around us, there is another world that we call supernatural. Elisha prayed for his servant, for him to see, 'that his eyes would be opened'. There is so much around us that we can't see with our natural eyes. We truly need God's help so that we can see again. Like in the days in the Garden of Eden when God use to come and visit us by the cool of the day, our eyes were seeing him and we were talking to him face to face. (We were created in Him from the foundations of the earth). That world is still here waiting for us. Yes, I am a witness of that.

2 Kings 6:17 And Elisha prayed, and said, "LORD, I pray, open his eyes that he may see." Then the LORD opened the eyes of the young man, and he saw. And behold, the mountain was full of horses and chariots of fire all around Elisha.

One day I was on the mountain next to John Robinson's house, at Alvensrus Farm in South Africa. I was praying and fasting for three days. At noon on the third day, the whole mountaintop was full of heavenly beings that were going from one end to the other. When they would get to the edge of the mountain, they would just keep walking. I thought that I was already there with the Father, out of the natural body but I was not. He came to be with me, as the promise says, come near to God and He will come near to you. When He came near to me, I was expecting another word from Him. None of them spoke to me. They were just displaying the heavens before me.

At that time, my desire was to wait and hear from them what they could tell me but I did not hear anything from them. I meditated there asking myself why are they just displaying the supernatural realm and not talking to me. While I was on that thought, a very heavy sleep started to overwhelm my mind. It overtook me and I suddenly fell asleep. I had a vision and in the vision, the Lord Himself started saying to me, "Why are you looking for another word? I gave you my word, I gave you faith, and I gave you my Spirit. I have shared with you whatever I could give. So take courage for I am with you. Use what you have." When I woke up all the heavenly beings were gone.

From that day, God began to increase his power. When I came down from the mountain, on Friday evening, I went to the church as usual, the angels appeared in the meeting, and the people did not want to leave the church that night, they stayed until the next day. One woman who was sick with AIDS was healed that night.

> Luke 9:1-2 [1] And He called the twelve together, and gave them power and authority over all the demons and to heal diseases. [2] And He sent them out to proclaim the kingdom of God and to perform healing. (NASB)

The Lord sends us to the all world so that we can operate in the same way using these gifts that he gave us. We need to ask and desire for the gifts. As the scriptures say, if we ask for bread he will not give us a stone.

Desire: The power of the will

> John 4:31-34 [31] In the meantime His disciples urged Him, saying, "Rabbi, eat." [32] But He said to them, **"I have food to eat of which you do not know."** [33] Therefore the disciples said to one another, "Has anyone brought Him anything to eat?" [34] Jesus said to them, "My food is to do the will of Him who sent me, and to finish His work.

Jesus rejected the food because His hunger and desire was to see the people repent and come to know Him. This was the will of His Father; for the people to know Him. He was hungry for righteousness, not for natural food. He was sustained, not by natural food, but by doing the will of the Father.

John 6:37-40   [37] All that the Father gives Me will come to Me, and the one who comes to Me I will by no means cast out. [38] For I have come down from heaven, not to do My **own will**, but the will of Him who sent Me. [39] This is the **will** of the Father who sent Me, that of all He has given Me I should lose nothing, but should raise it up at the last day. [40] **And this is the will of Him who sent Me**, that everyone who sees the Son and believes in Him may have everlasting life; and I will raise him up at the last day."

The plan that the Father has for humanity and His will for this world is that everyone would look to the Son and believe in Him. The Bible says, to all that receive him, he gives the power to become the children of God. The will and desire of the Father is that none would perish, but that everyone may have life through his Son, Jesus Christ.

Matthew 7:21 "Not everyone who says to Me, 'Lord, Lord,' shall enter the kingdom of heaven, but he who does the **will** of My Father in heaven.

The Father does not want to fill churches with people who simply sit and do nothing. His desire is that they do the will of The Father. It is not enough to simply believe without doing something; we must believe and then do something. Those who are preachers are very encouraged by this verse, but if a person is not doing the will of the Father this is the scariest verse in the Bible. Whatever we receive in the church is meant to point us to go to the field. When we are fed, we will reach out. The **will** of the Father is to point the people to Jesus, to look to him, believe in him and to have life. Not life for ourselves but for the entire world to be saved.

Matthew 6: 9-10
 [9] In this manner, therefore, pray:
  Our Father in heaven,
  Hallowed be Your name.
 [10] Your kingdom come.
  Your **will** be done
  On earth as it is in heaven.

The significance of the Kingdom that Jesus reveals is first to respect the name of the Father and second to call for His Kingdom to come. It is to find out that the Kingdom is righteousness, peace and joy in the Holy Spirit. When we call for righteousness, peace and joy, we will be able to do His will here on earth as it is in Heaven. It is difficult to do His will if we do not have His righteous, peace and joy. That is why Jesus says to exalt Him and call for His Kingdom. We must have God's Kingdom here on earth. When His Kingdom is on earth, the task of doing His will is easy for us.

Proclaim it now. Father, we glorify your name.
We praise You and love You.
You are The Prince of Peace, all Righteousness and Joy
unspeakable
We proclaim, your Kingdom – come! Peace – come!
Joy – come! Righteousness – come. Jesus – come!
Your will – be done on earth as it is in Heaven.
Let Your will be done in me.
Let Your Kingdom come in me. Amen.

Luke 22:42 saying, "Father, if it is Your will, take this cup away from Me; nevertheless not My will, but Yours, be done."

Jesus is our example, even though He had his personal will, He submitted it to the Father. The will of the Father found its perfection in His life. So, I find too, that it is very important for me to submit my will, so that the will of the Father can find its perfection in me. It is where we come up with the words "die-to-self", so that the will of the Father may find its perfection in our lives. When my will is strong, the Fathers' will becomes less. When His will is strong, my will becomes less. Spend time with Jesus; let Him feed you with His will. Let Him possess your mind with His will. Spend time with Him. The more we spend time with Him in prayer, our will become less and his will become strong. His will, will lead us to the goal of perfect submission to the Father.

Hebrews 10:9-10 [9] then He said, "Behold, I have come to do Your will, O God." He takes away the first *(the law)* that He may establish the second *(the will of the Father).* [10] By that will we have been sanctified through the offering of the body of Jesus Christ once for all.

Everyone has been called to live by the *law* but in Jesus, everyone is now called to live by his perfect *will.* The second became satisfied through Christ, which is his perfect *will.* His *will* was for the Son to die on the cross and to save the world and the first was for the people to live by the *law.* The second was for us to live by his *will,* which is to take Jesus into our lives and live by him.

Matthew 12:50 For whoever does the **will** of My Father in heaven is My brother and sister and mother."

Mark 3:35 For whoever does the **will** of God is My brother and My sister and mother."

Jesus came to unite us to the Father. That we may all become one, serving him, hearing his word and keeping his word. He came that we may serve together in oneness and unity. Therefore, we become one with God, when we receive Him into our lives.

The Daily Bread

Jesus said to pray to give us today our daily bread. We should be expectant of daily revelation from the Lord. The Holy Spirit will give us a new song. He will give us that daily revelation when we are expectant.

Luke 11:3-4
[3]Give us day by day our daily bread.
[4]And forgive us our sins,
 For we also forgive everyone who is indebted to us.
 And do not lead us into temptation,
 But deliver us from the evil one."

In April 2001, I was at Zimpeto in Maputo. It was 5:00 o'clock in the morning and I saw a vision of a man with a bag and in the bag were bombs. He came to the Bible school and started distributing them to the people. He said, take this and go in to all the villages, and give them to all of the pastors. On the bomb was written the words "life and truth". Those bombs carried "life and truth." As those bombs were taken to the villages, the people were filled with "life and truth." I saw the people receiving those bombs running in all directions. The bombs started exploding and the

> All you have to do is trust God's revelation. God's revelation is your daily bread.

villages over-flowed with life and truth. Then the man came to me and said, "I want to tell you about trust. All you have to do is trust God's revelation. God's revelation is your daily bread."

The Peace Makers

Matthew 5:9 Blessed are the peacemakers: for they shall be called sons of God.

I have seen peacemakers in countries that have been in war like Mozambique, Congo and Angola…when soldiers from other countries would come in with very strong weapons and set peace in place.

Joshua 5:13-15   ¹³ And it came to pass, when Joshua was by Jericho, that he lifted his eyes and looked, and behold, a Man stood opposite him with His sword drawn in His hand. And Joshua went to Him and said to Him, "Are You for us or for our adversaries?"
¹⁴ So He said, "No, but as Commander of the army of the LORD I have now come." And Joshua fell on his face to the earth and worshiped, and said to Him, "What does my Lord say to His servant?"
¹⁵ Then the Commander of the LORD'S army said to Joshua, "Take your sandal off your foot, for the place where you stand is holy." And Joshua did so.

Joshua was in a difficult time. He needed peace. In pressing in for that peace, the Man of peace came and stood beside him. He asked a simple question, "Are you for us or against us?" Joshua realized that he could ask this Man this question. He knew that this Man knew everything. He knew what was happening on both sides.

The man standing there knew Joshua was in a battle. Joshua knew that this man was strong. Seeing the Man in front of him, he looked like a formidable warrior. Joshua was given the opportunity to appeal with the Man, which is why he asked, "Are you for us or against us?" The Man, knowing his mission, answered correctly. The Man declared God's mission, not Joshua's mission, nor his enemy's mission. God's mission is to help those that are in need of help, to give hope to those that are hopeless, to strengthen the weak, to provide for those who do not have anything, to feed those that are hungry. He needed to see the hunger of Joshua. That is why the Man answered Joshua's question. He says, "No", I'm not *for* you,

I'm not *against* you, but as Commander of God's army, I am a rescuer of the weak.

Immediately when Joshua heard that he had a choice to make, to pursue the peace or to reject the peace, he chose to pursue the peace and immediately he bowed down with his face to the ground in submission. He put himself in the position of hopelessness, as someone that is desperate for help. He knew that the battle belonged to this Man and that peace belongs to him as well. So, he bowed his face to the ground not even wanting to look at the Man. He completely gave himself to the Commander of the Lord's army. Joshua is saying, here I am, do whatever is pleasing to you, I bow down in submission to peace. The Commander of the Lord's army wanted to see if Joshua was going to be obedient to what he was going to say. That is why he said take off your shoes, because the place you are is holy. Joshua did so in submission to The Peacemaker.

I believe that a peacemaker is anyone that comes to help in whatever struggle you are facing. If you are demon-possessed and someone does deliverance with you, the person who helps you, becomes a peacemaker. Because we believe, no demon can chase another demon away, whoever comes and chases the demon away from you… that is a peacemaker. If you are fighting with a sickness and someone comes and lays hands on you, and healing comes… that is a peacemaker. If you are dead and someone comes prays for you and you are raised from the dead… that is also a peacemaker. The children of God do all these things. To be a peacemaker you have to be a warrior, you have to have spiritual weapons.

Ephesians 6:13 Therefore put on the full armor of God, so that when the day of evil comes, you may be able to stand your ground, and after you have done everything, to stand. (NIV)

1 Peter 3:10-11 [10] For, "The one who desires life, to love and see good days, Must keep his tongue from evil and his lips from speaking deceit. [11] "He must turn away from evil and do well; He must seek **peace** and pursue it. (NASB)

How good it is to have an encounter with Jesus because He is Peace Himself. To seek peace is to come near to Him and He will come to us because He loves us more than His own life.

Chapter 5

How to Have a Good Day

Isaiah 29:19
The humble also shall increase their **joy** in the LORD, and the poor among men shall rejoice in the Holy One of Israel.

Most of us think that when we have many material things we will rejoice. Isaiah points people to the true defining purpose in life. That purpose is "In the Lord!" Joy is released to the poor and humble and their joyful destiny is not found in material possessions, but rather in Him. It is in Him that He brings us to a place of ongoing joy!

Habakkuk 3:18 Yet I will rejoice in the LORD, I will **joy** in the God of my salvation.

Habakkuk has just walked through a very painful experience in his own life. His choice was to turn to God and rejoice in Him, regardless of the negative circumstances he was enduring. He found his joy in trusting God, it was a joy of trust, no matter what came against him. We have that

51

capability in the midst of pain or negative circumstances as well.

> Romans 14:17 for the kingdom of God is not eating and drinking, but righteousness and peace and **joy** in the Holy Spirit.

> 1 Chronicles 15:16 Then David spoke to the leaders of the Levites to appoint their brethren to be the singers accompanied by instruments of music, stringed instruments, harps, and cymbals, by raising the voice with resounding **joy**.

Joy and worship work together. If you lose your joy, you lose your focus. When you lose your focus, it is easy to become a target by the enemy, and without the joy you will not have the strength to win the battle. King David set an example for us of how we can live. We can walk into life with joy regardless of our circumstances, and continue worshipping in the midst of those circumstances. Because when you lose your joy, you lose your trust. We must trust in the Lord always. This is how we can have a good day.

> **Trust in the Lord always and you will have a good day.**

> Nehemiah 8:10 Then he said to them, "Go your way, eat the fat, drink the sweet, and send portions to those for whom nothing is prepared; for this day is holy to our Lord. Do not sorrow, for the **joy** of the LORD is your strength."

When we compare the accomplishments of Nehemiah and Ezra, the differences are obvious. Ezra, the priest, rebuilt the walls of Jerusalem with tears, and the result was a very long and drawn out effort. When Nehemiah, the prophet, rebuilt the walls, he did it joyfully and received strength to complete it quickly. The joy of the Lord provided them the strength to accomplish the task before them. If you want to do something for God, do it with joy, because if you do it with tears you will be frustrated, but with joy you will accomplish it because you will have so much strength.

> Psalms 5:11 But let all those rejoice who put their trust in You; Let them ever shout for **joy**, because You defend them; Let those also who love Your name be **joy**ful in You.

> Psalms 16:11 You will show me the path of life;
> In Your presence is fullness of **joy**;
> At Your right hand are pleasures forevermore.

If you want to carry the presence of God, you can do it with joy, because in His presence is fullness of joy. Therefore, God is calling his people to come into His presence to experience His joy and to receive His joy.

> Psalms 32:11 Be glad in the LORD and rejoice, you righteous; and shout for **joy**, all you upright in heart!

> Psalms 33:3 Sing to Him a new song;
> Play skillfully with a shout of **joy**.

> Psalms 51:8 Make me hear **joy** and gladness,
> *That* the bones You have broken may rejoice.

> Psalms 51:12 Restore to me the **joy** of Your salvation,
> And uphold me *by Your* generous Spirit.

> Psalms 105:43 He brought out His people with **joy**,

His chosen ones with gladness.

Because he knew very well the new ways of worship, David clearly understood God's joy. He knew that the living God needed to see joy in the faces of his children. When God saves us, from our inner being joy bubbles up into wells of living water. It is a promise He has given to us.

Isaiah 12:3 Therefore with **joy** you will draw water
From the wells of salvation.

Isaiah 35:10 and Isaiah 51:11
And the ransomed of the LORD shall return,
And come to Zion with singing,
With everlasting **joy** on their heads.
They shall obtain **joy** and gladness,
And sorrow and sighing shall flee away.

Isaiah 65:18 But be glad and rejoice forever in what I create; For behold, I create Jerusalem as a rejoicing, And her people a **joy**.

Isaiah 60:5 Then you shall see and become radiant,
And your heart shall swell with **joy**;
Because the abundance of the sea shall be turned to you,
The wealth of the Gentiles shall come to you.

God's promise to us is everlasting joy. His promise is gladness and freedom from sorrow and worry. His promise is the abundance of His inheritance poured out over us. His promise to us is to be a joyful people.

Isaiah 61:3 To console those who mourn in Zion
To give them beauty for ashes,
The oil of **joy** for mourning,
The garment of praise for the spirit of heaviness;
That they may be called trees of righteousness,
The planting of the LORD, that He may be glorified."

Isaiah 61:7 Instead of your shame *you shall have* double
honor and *instead* of confusion they shall rejoice in their
portion. Therefore in their land they shall possess double;
Everlasting **joy** shall be theirs.

Everlasting joy is our inheritance. While the children
of Israel were coming out of Egypt, they experienced small
"clips" of joy. God's intention was for them to have everlasting
joy; a joy that would last forever.

Jeremiah 31:13 "Then shall the virgin rejoice in the dance,
And the young men and the old, together;
For I will turn their mourning to **joy**, will comfort them,
And make them rejoice rather than sorrow.

Jeremiah 33:9 Then it shall be to Me a name of **joy**, a
praise, and an honor before all nations of the earth, who
shall hear all the good that I do to them; they shall fear
and tremble for all the goodness and all the prosperity that
I provide for it.'

Jesus Christ carries the name 'joy.' He is our joy. The
whole earth is meant to know the joy that can be found in
Jesus. For when they find Him, they will find joy.

Acts 2:28 You have made known to me the ways of life;
You will make me full of **joy** in Your presence.'

Matthew 2:10 When they saw the star, they rejoiced with exceedingly great **joy**.

Matthew 25:21 His lord said to him, "Well *done*, good and faithful servant; you were faithful over a few things, I will make you ruler over many things. Enter into the **joy** of your lord.'

The invitation of God stands. He calls us to always be faithful and to enter into His joy. What are you waiting for? Enter into the joy of the Lord!

Luke 1:44 For indeed, as soon as the voice of your greeting sounded in my ears, the babe leaped in my womb for **joy**.

Luke 2:10 Then the angel said to them, "Do not be afraid, for behold, I bring you good tidings of great **joy** which will be to all people.

The message of Jesus is great joy. He is the message of joy, not only for the Jew but also for all the people all over the world.

John 15:11 "These things I have spoken to you, that My **joy** may remain in you, and *that* your **joy** may be full."

John 16:24 Until now you have asked nothing in My name. Ask, and you will receive, that your **joy** may be full.

To enter into the fullness of God's joy, we must understand how Jesus provides for that. He says that when we ask in his name he would give it to us, so that He would see the joy in us. He said that we don't have because we don't ask. If we ask, we will receive joy and our joy will be full.

> John 17:13 But now I come to You, and these things I speak in the world, that they may have My **joy** fulfilled in themselves.

> Romans 14:17 for the kingdom of God is not eating and drinking, but righteousness and peace and **joy** in the Holy Spirit.

> Romans 15:13 Now may the God of hope fill you with all **joy** and peace in believing, that you may abound in hope by the power of the Holy Spirit.

> Galations 5:22 But the fruit of the Spirit is love, **joy**, peace, longsuffering, kindness, goodness, faithfulness,

For a long time I have been looking to see who has good days? I looked at the rich people. They have many earthly treasures but I found out that they are not having good days; in fact, some have a hard time sleeping well. Even with all of their possessions, those possessions don't bring them joy.

I went to the poor and downcast to see if they were having a good time and good days. What I found was that they too seemed to have much to worry about and were having a hard time sleeping.

I said to myself, "Blessed are those that have received Him because they have so much joy, that no matter their circumstances, the joy of the Lord is their strength." Ten pastors can minister to one demon possessed person, trying to cast out the demon with tears of sorrow, and that demon will laugh over them. Actually, this is exactly what the demon wants. He does not want the people to have joy. He has come to steal, destroy and to kill. First, he makes sure he has stolen your joy. Then he comes to destroy your body. Finally, he comes to kill. So start regaining your strength, if you want to cast out a demon, rejoice in your God. Trust Him because when you have joy you will trust. When you laugh, the demon will cry, and you will cast out the demon with all authority. He will go into dry places with his tears and you will remain with the joy of the Lord as your strength.

This joy is yours to ask for. What are you waiting for?

Chapter 6

Visions and Dreams

One Friday evening while I was in Satellite Beach, Florida at Pastor Larry Booth's house, I had a vision. The One Who Is Life came to me on that date and showed me this vision. I pray that the Lord will bless you as you read this as He demonstrates how alive He is to you. Wow!

After the service we were talking in the house and I said to Pastor Larry that I was tired and needed to get some sleep. I went into the bedroom where I was staying. I crawled into bed and switched off the light. Then I laid down to go to sleep. Immediately it felt like someone came into the room, and turned the light on; even though my eyes were still closed.

I opened my eyes to see what was happening but when I did; I found out that I was not in the house. I was in the place beside a Mansion, there were many people, and every one was busy preparing the Banquet.

There was someone standing next to me, very gentle looking and he said to me this is my Wedding that is getting

59

ready so I am waiting for the Ring. As soon He said that, another person came to us where we were standing, bringing a ring that was very small. As soon as I saw the ring, I said, "No Lord, you have to get another ring because this ring is too small; no one will fit into this." Then He said to me "I want my bride to become as a little Child and this ring will fit her."

Mark 10:15 Assuredly, I say to you, whoever does not receive the kingdom of God as a little child will by no means enter it.

I cried and asked for forgiveness. I said to Him, "Please forgive me if there is pride in me Lord." He responded, "Okay, now let us go to the Gate. I want to show you the gate that I spoke of in Luke 13:24 where I said 'Strive to enter through the narrow gate, for many, I say to you, will seek to enter and will not be able.' "

He took me to the gate and it was very narrow. In measuring it, it was one foot wide and three feet high and again, I started crying and said to Him "Please forgive me!" He said, "Okay, then let us go to the city. I want to show you what is happening there!" As we were going, I was very happy to go and see the City. When we arrived next to it, I started seeing a very strange thing. The city was very beautiful but the people in it were strange looking, as if all of them were working with a tree in their head. I said, "Lord what is this?" and he said, "What you see is the seed of the tree of knowledge of good and evil that has grown in the mind of this people."

Genesis 3:4-5 [4] Then the serpent said to the woman, "You will not surely die. [5] For God knows that in the day you eat of it your eyes will be opened, and you will be like God, knowing good and evil."

Daniel said that knowledge would increase. They are striving to grow that tree. It will be difficult for them to enter through the Narrow Gate. I tell you, the only poison that will kill this tree is Humility.

> Daniel 12:4 "But you, Daniel, shut up the words, and seal the book until the time of the end; many shall run to and fro, and knowledge shall increase."

> Philippians 2:5-8 [5] Let this mind be in you which was also in Christ Jesus, [6] who, being in the form of God, did not consider it robbery to be equal with God, [7] but made Himself of no reputation, taking the form of a bondservant, *and* coming in the likeness of men. [8]And being found in appearance as a man, He humbled Himself and became obedient to *the point of* death, even the death of the cross.

The tree will die, even from its root by Humility, so therefore humble yourself under the mighty hand of God that He may lift you up. After that, I couldn't move from the place where I was standing, so He came and carried me and brought me back to the room. It was 4:00 am. When I returned to the room, I started praying until sunrise; I was not tired.

> **The only poison that will kill this tree is Humility.**

> Psalms 45:4 And in Your majesty ride prosperously because of truth, humility, *and* righteousness; And Your right hand shall teach You awesome things.

An End Time Vision

I was at home praying on September 25, 2006. Suddenly I was taken to a place where I met many people standing in one line waiting for the Lord to come. The time was 11:45 pm. The rain started pouring out and the people started coming out of the waiting line. They were running away from the rain. I pleaded with the people to wait for the Master. "In just a few minutes, the Master is coming" I told them. Only a few people remained in the line. I knelt down and began crying to the Lord about being the only one here. Then, as I was beseeching the Lord, someone touched my shoulder. I looked and it was Benny Hinn and he said to me you are not alone, "Look who is coming." When I raised my eyes to see there was a multitude of people coming from every way and they were all dressed in white. I had never met Benny before but spiritually I now have. (Thank you Benny Hinn, may the Lord bless you. Amen.)

A Vision of Worship

We were in a meeting in Houston, Texas worshiping the Living God, the creator of Heaven and Earth. I was in intense worship, reading my Bible and asking for the Word before preaching. We were singing "You are Holy, You are Holy, You are Holy our God." As we worshipped Him, it became very intense and the atmosphere became thick with His Presence. A cloud started gathering and a thick rain began to pour down. It was not a rain of water but the rain of the precious stones; the colors were green, grey, blue, purple, yellow and clear. There were a lot of gemstones, diamonds and gold falling. Precious gold and diamonds became so intense that the people that were with me in the worship became distracted with those things and started gathering the diamonds and jewels into their bags.

I stayed on my knees and continued worshipping with my hands held high. A friend came and said to me "Don't you know that everyone is busy gathering the blessing … here are some diamonds." He put them in my hand but I continued worshipping with my eyes closed and my heart focused on the One that lives forever. At that time, the people started dancing a mercy celebration of the blessing. I was still on my knees worshiping and singing "You are awesome, You are awesome, You are awesome our God." Suddenly, there was a great light shining all around. It was so real that you could touch it. I raised my hands up to the light, it touched my fingers, and my body started changing into the likeness of the light. A few who were in worship and some others saw it too. They realized that it was very important to join in the worship, and so they joined the worship again in repentance and they were healed of many diseases. The first who returned to focus on worshipping Him, became like the light. Those who delayed and were distracted remained the same as they were before. The fear of the Lord came upon them all and the light was shining from the earth to the sky. The refrain of that song continues constantly in my mind:

> "You are Holy,
> You are Holy,
> You are Holy our God".

John 4:24 God *is* Spirit, and those who worship Him must worship in spirit and truth.

Exodus 34:14 --for you shall not worship any other god, for the LORD, whose name is Jealous, is a jealous God-- (NASB)

Psalm 66:4 All the earth shall worship You

　　And sing praises to You;

　　They shall sing praises *to* Your name." Selah

Exodus 9:13b ... This is what the LORD, the God of the Hebrews, says: Let my people go, so that they may worship me, (NIV)

Exodus 23:25 Worship the LORD your God, and his blessing will be on your food and water. I will take away sickness from among you, (NIV)

Revelation 14:7 He said in a loud voice, "Fear God and give him glory, because the hour of his judgment has come. Worship him who made the heavens, the earth, the sea and the springs of water." (NIV)

Hebrews 12:28 Therefore, since we are receiving a kingdom that cannot be shaken, let us be thankful, and so worship God acceptably with reverence and awe, (NIV)

Revelation 4:8-11   [8]Each of the four living creatures had six wings and was covered with eyes all around, even under his wings. Day and night they never stop saying: "Holy, holy, holy is the Lord God Almighty, who was, and is, and is to come." [9]whenever the living creatures give glory, honor and thanks to him who sits on the throne and who lives for ever and ever, [10]the twenty-four elders fall down before him who sits on the throne, and worship him who lives forever and ever. They lay their crowns before the throne and say:

[11] "You are worthy, our Lord and God,

　　to receive glory and honor and power,

　　for you created all things,

and by your will they were created
and have their being." (NIV)

We are created to worship our living God. We are called to worship him, no matter what our circumstances. Throughout the Bible, it speaks about worshipping God with a sincere heart, without hypocrisy. Most of us worship God because its part of our religion. What God really wants from us is for us to worship Him, not because it's a part of our religion but because He is our true Father. We are created to say, "Thank you!" for whatever He does for us. I have seen the Presence of God fall and heal people when they are simply worshipping. In fact, at most of our crusades the people experience complete healing during worship.

One day when we were in intense worship, I saw a rushing wind come into our building and the color of the building was changed. The wind was circling in the building. Some of the people in the building were manifesting in very different ways, some were laughing, falling, some were prophesying and some receiving healing by themselves. Almost everyone that was in the room received one of these manifestations. That day our service was completely changed, no one had the strength to go and preach because the Holy Spirit was controlling the meeting. We remained in intense worship the whole day and when the manifestation was cooling down it was already quite late for someone to preach -- we simply obeyed the Holy Spirit. That day the people learned more then when we have had a preacher in the pulpit. The following Sunday almost everyone brought a friend, a new believer to the church, they became doers of the word. This is what God is saying in our days -- he has so many songs for us to sing. My prayer is that this generation and the generations to come, will have their songs to sing for him. As the Bible says 'sing to the Lord a new song' and this is what he is asking of us, seek for new songs that speak about him. I am not saying that it is not good to sing the old songs or old hymns, we can sing them, but we must also write our new songs. We must not abide in old generation revelations; if God spoke to them he will speak to us; He is the same God yesterday, today and forever. He never keeps silent to those who come to him and ask him for something.

Vision of Sand and Fire

One November I was sitting on a chair praying. Suddenly I saw a bunch of sand before me, and on the sand there was fire and the sand increased. The more the sand increased the more the fire increased. The sand increased in all directions along with the fire. There was a wall around the sand and fire and then the fire was opening the doors on the walls. It was opening the doors for the flowing of the sand. All the doors in different areas were being opened. Wherever the fire went, the doors were opened. After the vision disappeared, I realized that it was the multitude of people, like the sand of the sea, that were on fire for God. The fire is going to open the doors for them, and the fire is going to lead them in the Way.

Vision Regarding the Final Lightning:

On January 12th and 13th, 2007, I had a vision while in deep prayer for California. I landed at San Francisco Airport and was nauseated to the point of feeling I could vomit. This continued all Thursday and Friday. After the Friday evening service, I started praying into the situation more in depth. I wanted revelation about what was happening. This is when the Lord took me into this vision:

"We started seeing the strange thing that was happening in the sky. There were a few people with me.

I saw layers of clouds. The first layer was black in color. Immediately, the scientists were taking that portion of the layer to study it. They gave the results of their study to public television, but the results made it in favor of Christians. Because Christians knew what was going on, without studying it, they knew the cloud meant what the scientists were saying.

As the media previewed the results of the study, they were sitting and discussing how they were going to distribute this information because it was in favor of Christians. They tried to twist the information and give a wrong result to the people. However, they were not able to twist the results.

At the same time, another layer of cloud was forming. It was a grayish red. People started dying as that cloud was coming. It was as if this cloud was sucking the blood of the people. Oxygen was not getting to them. They were withering up quickly as their blood dried in their veins, but Christians were not dying. Again, the scientists studied the layer. As they were doing this study, it was coming to the same point of favor for the Christians. Again, the scientists saw in the study, that at the edge of the cloud layers there was another power – a supernatural power.

It was a strange and dunamis [dynamic] power that could generate electricity – greater than any power – it could even melt the whole earth. The power was lightning; a very great and strange lightning that would cause great damage on the earth. After the lightning, the earth is going to be changed. Every living creature is going to be changed – it is not going to be the same again.

The scientists were saying that possibly every being is going to change into another being. They say nothing will remain the same after the final lightning. Again, they gave the report to the media.

Then another layer was coming and that cloud was a pale cloud. This cloud was very strong and warm. As the cloud moved slowly, everything under the cloud was dying.

Some of the scientists were starting to get frustrated, and so they began to make a plan against Christians. In all the high places, all the plans they were making were against Christianity. They now viewed these things as happening because Christians were causing them to happen.

As they were making their plans, another layer was coming – that layer was very white, like a veil for a wedding. That layer was a rescue to cover the Christians, because the others were planning to destroy all Christianity. As soon as that layer came, again, the scientists made a test on that layer – and then they became even more frustrated.

Some of the scientists committed suicide; some started looking to Christians for another plan. It seems like God was making the foolish things to be wiser than the 'wise' people. The people who were without shame but were looking for help, could get help from Christians.

Because of the media everybody was talking about the 'final lightning' – that is what they were calling it – the 'final lightning' – because they had already published that after the lightning came, everything would be changed.

While the veil was coming to rescue the Christians, the Christians went to the honey farm. When we arrived at the honey farm, there was a lot of honey – the whole farm was full of honey. It was hard to enjoy the honey because there were so many bees – aggressive bees that were stinging the people. There was not enough food for the people to eat unless they could eat the honey.

Then we started praying. I fell down with my face on the ground in worship of the LIVING GOD. While in this position, a fire started. When the fire started, the bees started fleeing. We started plundering the bees' honey. There was enough for everybody, for about three and a half years. When the people were celebrating in that feast of honey, the final lightning came. While the whole world was in great fear, we Christians started singing and dancing. We started dancing as though nothing was coming.

Then I heard a trumpet sound.

When the trumpet sounded – the lightning came and changed everything! When everything changed, even the minds of everybody who lived after the lightning, were not the same. Together with all other beings, we were in some place most glorious. We just sang songs of celebration! Amen!

When the vision disappeared, I didn't think I was in San Francisco, I thought I was somewhere else. After the vision, immediately, everything was over and I was no longer nauseated.

The Hand

In November 2004 at a Conference in Dondo I had an experience into the invisible world. The Spirit of God was on me as He was on most of the pastors that day. I started feeling as if someone was pouring buckets of water into my ears. It eventually got to the point where I could not hear the sound of the music and I was unable to think or remember. Suddenly I found myself walking toward a man seated in a place that was protected by something that looked like a house made of glass. I entered in and saw that it was Father Abraham seated there. He had a long white beard. He didn't look at me or into my eyes, he was looking somewhere else. Even though he was not looking at me, he knew my past, present and future. He knew everything that was and was to come. When I went into the house, I laid down right next to him and he stretched out his hand and touched my shoulder. He said to me, "My son, I want to tell you about the importance of God's hand."

2 Samuel 24:14 And David said to Gad, "I am in great distress. Please let us fall into the hand of the LORD, for His mercies *are* great; but do not let me fall into the hand of man."

Luke 23:46 And when Jesus had cried out with a loud voice, He said, "Father, *'into Your hands I commit My spirit.'* " Having said this, He breathed His last.

I saw the hand of the living God protecting David because he knew the importance of God's protection. As he was still talking to me, it was like, I was watching a real movie and he was narrating the events. Then he took me to the story of Jesus; to the week that Jesus was betrayed. He was having a conversation with the disciples, in which he was sharing about his death and resurrection. So he said to me, 'Look what happened to my Lord' and it was strange for me to hear Father Abraham call Jesus, 'My Lord'. As he continued to narrate the story, my eyes remained fixed on the events I was seeing. Abraham continued, "The Son of Man is about to be betrayed into the hands of men." (Matthew 17:22) As I heard these words, I was watching it unfold before my eyes on Jesus.

I was back in the time of Jesus on the earth. I saw the whole story again. I saw when they arrested Him. I saw him being beating. I watched Him being spit upon and He could not do anything because He was in the hands of men. I was afraid of them but He encouraged me, saying, "I want to show you the prize that purchased your life. You were bought with a great price and your life is precious to the Father."

Luke 23:46 And when Jesus had cried out with a loud voice, He said, "Father, *'into Your hands I commit My spirit.'* " Having said this, He breathed His last.

The same hand that had protected David was being outstretched to Jesus while He was enduring such pain.

Matthew 22:44 'The LORD said to my Lord,
  "Sit at My right hand,
  Till I make Your enemies Your footstool"'?

Immediately the sun got dark, it started lightning and thundering, the earth began to quake and the true fear of the Lord fell on those people that were mistreating my Lord, and joy came to me as I looked and saw the Son of God sitting at the right hand of the Mighty One. Then father Abraham spoke to me...

1 Peter 5:6 Therefore humble yourselves under the mighty hand of God, that He may exalt you in due time,

Matthew 17:12 But I say to you that Elijah has come already, and they did not know him but did to him whatever they wished. Likewise the Son of Man is also about to suffer at their hands.

Luke 22:69 Hereafter the Son of Man will sit on the right hand of the power of God."

Mark 12:36 For David himself said by the Holy Spirit:
  "The LORD said to my Lord,
  'Sit at My right hand,
  Till I make Your enemies Your footstool.' "

This Hand protected David. This Hand reached out to Jesus. This same Hand is reaching out to us right now. He will hold us by you by your right hand. "For I am the LORD, your God, who takes hold of your right hand and says to you, Do not fear; I will help you. Do not be afraid, O worm Jacob, O little Israel, for I myself will help you," declares the LORD, your Redeemer, the Holy One of Israel. (Isaiah 41:13-14)

Chapter 7

The Rush Hour

Vision of the fruit

A preacher from America was teaching about prayer. During the meeting, a man was jumping up and down on one foot. He went over to him and asked the man what was going on with him? The man answered him that he couldn't control himself. The preacher said to the jumping man, "Are you a believer?" He replied, "Yes". "Do you know the Bible?" the preacher asked. "Yes", the man answered. Then the preacher said to him, "You are not a believer and you do not know the Bible, because the Bible says that 'the fruit of the Spirit is self-control.' How can you not be able to control yourself right now if you are a believer?"

I was worried. My faith was in question because I am like that sometimes. I cannot control myself. I went home sad, thinking that I was not pleasing God. It was 4:45 pm East African time when I got home. I went to my room, knelt down, and started to pray, seeking God's guidance about this matter.

While I prayed, I started feeling what felt like someone pouring a bucket of water into my ear. I tried to bring myself under control. Instead, I was losing my power to control my reactions to this experience. I thought, "Just let me kill my mind," as all this stuff was happening. I opened my eyes yet I do not know if those were my two eyes or new ones. I found myself in the most holy presence of the Ancient of Days, the One that lives forever and ever. His appearance was indescribable. It was very quiet and there before the Ancient of Days were unnumbered heavenly beings all prostrated with their face down toward the Ancient of Days. I asked, "Why is it so quiet up here and where is the glory?" The Ancient of Days answered, "You have the glory you have to give the glory to us." I said to myself this is my imagination and the Ancient of Days said to me, "Without flesh and blood there is no imagination". I said, "Indeed, I do not have flesh and blood with me." I started to touch my body and it was like I was trying to hold the wind. I started thinking to myself, "I had heard that people came up here with their earthly bodies." "Where are they?" The Ancient of Days did not say a word, he just turned his eyes to the side and my eyes following His. As I looked, at the end of God's side, I saw a garden and it was a most beautiful one. At the entrance of the garden, there was a gate. Inside the gate there were two people standing, they were looking and smiling at me.

As I saw them, I realized that I was holding nine fruits. It assumed that I had brought these from the earth. I began running to give them to the people that were inside the gate. Discernment rose in me that I needed to give the knowledge to the people standing in the gate. Elijah was closer than Enoch as I rushed to the gate to give them the fruit. The Ancient of Days rose his hand and said to me, "Stop do not go into the gate now; if you do you will not come out, and the fruit that you have is not for them. That fruit is for your brothers down there where you are coming from and for yourself. Share love with your brothers and as you share, use also self-control for your good".

He continued, "Go back and tell the harvesters to go into the fields in a rush. They have to reap while it is day and while there is still enough time because a bad wind is coming. This is the wind of temptation and it is going to destroy the crops. While it is ripe, harvest it."

I asked the Lord, "How?" He said to me, "Remember the gifts are coming. They will control you and lead you and you will no longer control yourself or the gift."

Again, I said to him, "When, Lord?" Although He did not answer, but all those prostrated before Him spoke to me in one voice as they stood up to their feet. There was an orchestra of lightning's and thunders and earthquakes and a thick cloud was covering them. It was becoming too much for me to bear. I started crying, and then I came back to my senses and I was back in my room again.

John 9:4 I must work the works of Him who sent Me while it is day; *the* night is coming when no one can work.

They said, "Tell the harvesters to go into the fields in a rush. They must reap while it is day and still enough time because a bad wind is coming. This is the wind of temptation and it is going to destroy the crops. While it is ripe, harvest it."

Jesus answered, "Are there not twelve hours in the day? If anyone walks in the day, he does not stumble, because he sees the light of this world." John 11:9

Again He said, "Tell the harvesters to go into the fields in a rush. They must reap while it is day and still enough time because a bad wind is coming. This is the wind of temptation and it is going to destroy the crops. While it is ripe, harvest it."

John 12:35 Then Jesus said to them, "A little while longer the light is with you. Walk while you have the light, lest darkness overtake you; he who walks in darkness does not know where he is going.

Again He said, "Tell the harvesters to go into the fields in a rush. They must reap while it is day and still enough time because a bad wind is coming. This is the wind of temptation and it is going to destroy the crops. While it is ripe, harvest it."

Galations 6:10 Therefore, as we have opportunity, let us do good to all, especially to those who are of the household of faith.

"Tell the harvesters to go into the fields in a rush. They must reap while it is day and still enough time because a bad wind is coming. This is the wind of temptation and it is going to cause the crops to fall, they will be destroyed, and the crop will fail. While it is still ripe, rush and harvest it."

Chapter 8

The Importance of Communication

...With God

After the Creation, God came to talk and visit the man and his wife.

Genesis 1:29 And God said, "See, I have given you every herb *that* yields seed which *is* on the face of all the earth, and every tree whose fruit yields seed; to you it shall be for food.

Genesis 3:8 And they heard the sound of the LORD God walking in the garden in the cool of the day, and Adam and his wife hid themselves from the presence of the LORD God among the trees of the garden.

Genesis 3:9 Then the LORD God called to Adam and said to him, "Where *are* you?"

God's desire is to look after us, to keep us from going away from him, and to tell us what we should and should not do. He desires to talk to us and reveal his goodness. It is very important to talk to God and listen to his voice.

Genesis 22:18 In your seed all the nations of the earth shall be blessed, because you have obeyed My voice."

Later God talked with Abraham who listened to Him and obeyed.

Isaiah 28:23 Give ear and hear my voice,
Listen and hear my speech.

Right now, He is talking to you and me. We must listen to him as He speaks to us.

John 10:16 And other sheep I have which are not of this fold; them also I must bring, and they will hear My voice; and there will be one flock *and* one shepherd.

When Jesus indicated that His sheep would hear His voice, He was talking about those that give their lives to him. That includes not only the Jews but also the Gentiles that were coming to his kingdom.

John 10:27 My sheep hear My voice, and I know them, and they follow Me.

Followers of Jesus hear His voice; like Saul on the road to Damascus; like Cornelius and many others. He continues to speak in many ways now through his Son, Jesus.

Hebrews 1:2 *He* has in these last days spoken to us by His Son, whom He has appointed heir of all things, through whom also He made the worlds;

Revelation 3:20 Behold, I stand at the door and knock. If anyone hears My voice and opens the door, I will come in to him and dine with him, and he with Me.

A wonderful feast has been promised to those who hear His Voice. We are given the promise of dining with Jesus if we will hear His voice and open our hearts (understanding) to him. That dinner begins here on Earth. It is the dinner of His goodness (righteousness, peace, and joy in the Holy Spirit). As we allow Him into our minds and commit our lives to live for him here on Earth, He gives us this meal.

...At home

The plan of the enemy is to bring division, even in our homes. It is a strategy that he uses to disable us from doing what God has called us to do. We must communicate in our homes. If our family does not talk with each other, we will feel separated from one another. I have found that this is the enemy's plan to keep people apart; he first slows down and starts eliminating their communication so that the relationship is weakened. Communication is what brings people together to share ideas and develop relationship. God wants us to communicate with one another, enjoy each other, and have a good time together.

...At Business

In the business workplace, it is also the same. The less you have communication with your employer, the more you feel disconnected. The more you communicate, the more everyone works towards the same goals. It is good to flow towards the same goals with your boss and employees.

...At Church

Even in the churches, people feel neglected from everybody because of a lack of communication.

When I was a youth I went to visit a church, and we were holding meetings under the mango trees. The service was wonderful. By the end of the meeting, it started to rain and all the people start running to their homes. They left me alone there under the tree waiting for the rain to stop. Nobody was there for me to talk to, I felt neglected, and I did not feel welcome in that place.

Now that I am a pastor, I know how it is to feel neglected. Therefore, my desire is to train the whole Church to carry the same burden of welcoming everyone that the body of Christ may feel at home.

Chapter 9

The Example of Peter's Life

One of the Disciple's had a life that was like the journey-of-life. He was invited by Jesus to become a fisher of men. He was later told that he was a rock… a pillar in the building of Jesus' Church… his name is Peter. He had so many failures in his life. Jesus called him, and what He called him to was wonderful. Peter's failures were not the end of the story, but the story is rather about God's faithfulness that would transform a simple fisherman to become one of the most powerful disciples.

…go for it

Mathew 4:18-20   [18] And Jesus, walking by the Sea of Galilee, saw two brothers, Simon called Peter, and Andrew his brother, casting a net into the sea; for they were fishermen. [19] Then He said to them, "Follow Me, and I will make you fishers of men." [20]They immediately left *their* nets and followed Him.

Peter began marching to the goal of his destiny as soon as he was called. The moment you hear the call of your destiny, go for it.

...step out of the boat

> Mathew 14:28-29 [28] And Peter answered Him and said, "Lord, if it is You, command me to come to You on the water." [29] So He said, "Come" And when Peter had come down out of the boat, he walked on the water to go to Jesus.

When Peter questioned Jesus, it was with excitement that he asked if he could walk on the water. He knew that everything would be okay as long as he was with Jesus. If we have Jesus, we can go where it seems impossible in the eyes of man. Jesus invited Peter to come out on the water. Jesus desires that we enjoy the supernatural realm with him. With your eyes fixed on Jesus, step out of the boat.

...the Rock

> Mathew 16:16-18 [16] Simon Peter answered and said, "You are the Christ, the Son of the living God."
> [17] Jesus answered and said to him, "Blessed are you, Simon Bar-Jonah, for flesh and blood has not revealed *this* to you, but My Father who is in heaven. [18] And I also say to you that you are Peter *[stone]*, and on this rock *[Petra, large stone]* I will build My church, and the gates of Hades shall not prevail against it.

Peter's life carried on in the supernatural because he knew what many others did not know. He knew how to draw from the *well*... the *well* of divine revelation... the *well* of hearing God's voice. He knew who Jesus was but that knowledge did not come from a book or the latest "tape-of-the month club". Peter received it straight from Heaven and his answer was right to the point. Jesus is the Anointed One and God is alive and saves through his Son.

Jesus later revealed what would be the foundation of the church. He revealed that it was a *'rock'* on which He would build His church. *Peter*, translated *'stone,'* in John 1:42 is a small rock. *Petra*, the large rock, is the foundation of divine revelation. It is the rock of hearing God's voice; it is the rock of being taught all things by the Holy Spirit. Peter gets it. Peter knew that the Church of Jesus Christ would be built on this rock of revelation and the floods and storms could not destroy it.

...overconfidence

> Mathew 16:22 Then Peter took Him aside and began to rebuke Him, saying, "Far be it from You, Lord; this shall not happen to You!"

Overconfidence can distort our ability to continue walking in true revelation. After the wonderful revelation that Peter had about Jesus, he crossed the threshold of pride and error would come out of his mouth.

Jesus began speaking to the disciples about His mission on earth, His death and resurrection. Because of the previous correct revelation about Jesus, Peter becomes overly confident and disagrees with the Lord; the One that made him walk on the water. Humanity took control of his life. He thought that he was doing well in life by turning to advise the Lord. But over confidence led him to not draw from the well, but his own emotions. He wasn't hearing from God at that time.

...correction

> Mathew 16:23   But He turned and said to Peter, "Get behind Me, Satan! You are an offense to Me, for you are not mindful of the things of God, but the things of men."

The response of Jesus is quick. The Lord saw right through the words and the heart and knew that it was the enemy that was influencing Peter, and He rebuked satan. How quickly Peter went from true revelation from Heaven of who Jesus was, back to his own [worldly influenced] reasoning.

...awkward moments

> Mathew 17:4 Then Peter answered and said to Jesus, "Lord, it is good for us to be here; if You wish, let us make here three tabernacles: one for You, one for Moses, and one for Elijah."

Peter's awkwardness with the supernatural is a good picture for us all to consider. In the Transfiguration with Jesus, Elijah, and Moses; Peter was so enjoying the world of supernatural, that he didn't include himself in the event! He wanted three shelters made for Jesus, Elijah, and Moses, but they weren't the only ones there! The supernatural is often very awkward, and we don't know how to react or respond to it. Many times like Peter, we can say things that are not important when God does supernatural things.

...promise of faithfulness

> Mathew 26:33 Peter answered and said to Him, "Even if all are made to stumble because of You, I will never be made to stumble."

Mathew 26:35 Peter said to Him, "Even if I have to die with You, I will not deny You!"

Jesus was everything to Peter. His promise to Jesus was as much as he could have at that time. He wanted the Lord to know that he was with Him and that he had given away everything for him. His life is not worth living by himself that he chooses to live for Him.

...he who has ears to hear...

John 18:10 Then Simon Peter, having a sword, drew it and struck the high priest's servant, and cut off his right ear. The servant's name was Malchus.

The reactions of Peter are very sudden. Peter thought that to die for Jesus also meant that he had to fight to the death, so he attacked. The kingdom Jesus taught for three and a half years had nothing to do with fighting, but about hearing and doing what the Father says. Peter cut off the ear of the servant of the high priest. He cut the ear because he saw that the Pharisee's had ears to hear but they didn't want to hear. As the Bible says, "he who has the ear let him hear what the spirit is saying." Jesus healed his ear. It was Jesus' final healing miracle. He did this to show the people and to show Peter that the **ear** in the last days is very important --- to hear.

...failed promises

Mathew 26:58 But Peter followed Him at a distance to the high priest's courtyard. And he went in and sat with the servants to see the end.

Mathew 26:69 Now Peter sat outside in the courtyard. And a servant girl came to him, saying, "You also were with Jesus of Galilee.

Luke 22:58 And after a little while another saw him and said, "You also are of them." But Peter said, "Man, I am not!"

Peter's promises to Jesus are about to begin being broken. The first failure of Peter was to deny Jesus when he promised to die with him. But even though Peter failed in his promises, Jesus' promise never fails. His promise to us will never fail. It will remain forever.

...words of life

John 6:68 But Simon Peter answered Him, "Lord, to whom shall we go? You have the words of eternal life.

Peter's failures led him to understand the importance of living with Jesus and that it is useless to live without Him. When he says, "Only you have the words of life." He was saying, "It is only when I am living with the Word of Life, I will have life.!"

...go where you go

John 13:36-37 [36] Simon Peter said to Him, "Lord, where are You going?" Jesus answered him, "Where I am going you cannot follow Me now, but you shall follow Me afterward." [37] Peter said to Him, "Lord, why can I not follow You now? I will lay down my life for Your sake."

Peter's love for Jesus draws him to want to go anywhere Jesus goes. He didn't realize that Jesus was talking about going to the cross. When Peter said that he will even lay his life down for Jesus sake. Even though he did not quite understand what Jesus was actually saying, Peter would eventually follow him, even to the point of dying on a cross.

...I am going fishing

> John 21:3 Simon Peter said to them, "I am going fishing." They said to him, "We are going with you also." They went out and immediately got into the boat, and that night they caught nothing.

Peter mobilized his friends to go back and fish. Jesus had said to them come, follow me and I will make you fishers of men. Peter forgot this promise of Jesus. They fished all night and caught nothing and in the morning, the Lord came to them to show them that he was still alive.

> John 21:7 Therefore that disciple whom Jesus loved said to Peter, "It is the Lord!" Now when Simon Peter heard that it was the Lord, he put on *his* outer garment (for he had removed it), and plunged into the sea.

> John 21:11 Simon Peter went up and dragged the net to land, full of large fish, one hundred and fifty-three; and although there were so many, the net was not broken.

Immediately when one of the disciples told him, that the Lord was waiting for him on the seashore, he remembered his unfaithfulness to him, he did not want to wait for the boat to reach the shore. He started swimming to meet the Lord, who was waiting for him. He was encouraged to see that Jesus was still alive and he immediately dropped everything and ran to him. As he was swimming to Jesus, he was probably thinking of all his failures but Jesus was looking at him as a great shepherd who was coming to meet him. After that meeting, he received another promise and he was given a commission to take care of His flock. Jesus continued to show His faithfulness to Peter and the disciples by telling them where they could catch fish. The Bible says that they caught 153 fish that day, and the net did not break. This miraculous catch was simply to show them that the Jesus they knew of yesterday was also the same Jesus of that day and forever.

...the restoration

> John 21:15-17   ¹⁵ So when they had eaten breakfast, Jesus said to Simon Peter, "Simon, *son* of Jonah, do you love Me more than these?" He said to Him, "Yes, Lord; You know that I love You." He said to him, "Feed My lambs."
> ¹⁶ He said to him again a second time, "Simon, *son* of Jonah, do you love Me?" He said to Him, "Yes, Lord; You know that I love You." He said to him, "Tend My sheep."
> ¹⁷ He said to him the third time, "Simon, *son* of Jonah, do you love Me?" Peter was grieved because He said to him the third time, "Do you love Me?" And he said to Him, "Lord, You know all things; You know that I love You." Jesus said to him, "Feed My sheep.

Peter is restored to the calling of God on his life. Three times Peter had denied Jesus on that early morning before the crucifixion. Three times Jesus asked Peter if he loved Him. Peter received back his responsibility and calling because when we repent to God, the Bible says He forgets our sins, and He uses us as if we had never sinned. He does not come reminding us of our past, if anyone is in Christ he is a new creation. So we must continue to renew our mind daily.

...stand up

Acts 1:15 And in those days Peter stood up in the midst of the disciples (altogether the number of names was about a hundred and twenty), and said,

Acts 2:14 But Peter, standing up with the eleven, raised his voice and said to them, "Men of Judea and all who dwell in Jerusalem, let this be known to you, and heed my words.

Stand up, take your place in Christ. Peter now takes back his authority. He is preaching to the people and is not remembering his past because the past was old. He pressed into his destiny, to be a fisher of men.

...the fruit

Acts 2:37-38 [37] Now when they heard *this*, they were cut to the heart, and said to Peter and the rest of the apostles, "Men *and* brethren, what shall we do?" [38] Then Peter said to them, "Repent, and let every one of you be baptized in the name of Jesus Christ for the remission of sins; and you shall receive the gift of the Holy Spirit.

Peter saw the fruit of being faithful, the people were coming in repentance, not coming to be condemned but to give their lives to Jesus. He was instructing them, pressing into his destiny of being a father, to feed the sheep.

...the gifts

Acts 3:6 Then Peter said, "Silver and gold I do not have, but what I do have I give you: In the name of Jesus Christ of Nazareth, rise up and walk."

The life of Peter continues to excel in the realm of the miraculous. The gifts that were operating in the life of Peter; as he carried the Name above all Names on his own life; that Name had a power to heal, to raise the dead, to set the captives free and to save.

...they have been with Jesus

Acts 3:11-12   [11]Now as the lame man who was healed held on to Peter and John, all the people ran together to them in the porch which is called Solomon's, greatly amazed.   [12] So when Peter saw *it*, he responded to the people: "Men of Israel, why do you marvel at this? Or why look so intently at us, as though by our own power or godliness we had made this man walk?

Acts 4:8 Then Peter, filled with the Holy Spirit, said to them, "Rulers of the people and elders of Israel:

Acts 5:29   But Peter and the *other* apostles answered and said: "We ought to obey God rather than men."

Acts 4:13 Now when they saw the boldness of Peter and John, and perceived that they were uneducated and untrained men, they marveled. And they realized that they had been with Jesus.

The boldness of Peter continues to grow. The man who had been the unfaithful, rejecter of Jesus, had a major change of direction. From the night when Jesus was arrested to the day he preached at Pentecost and three thousand were added to the church. This same Peter who mobilized his friends to leave and go fishing is now addressing the people about the power of

God, to be a witness of Jesus Christ who is still alive, he still heals, and the Holy Spirit was with him. The people were amazed to hear his message because he was so full of boldness. They marveled at a man who was so weak, who was now addressing them with these powerful things of God. Their conclusion is that this man had been with Jesus. As the Bible says, "who has the son of God has the testimony." The people saw the difference because they had experienced Jesus the Christ. If you have really been involved with Jesus and you drink of his Spirit you will never be the same again, because his Spirit changes lives. From the day Peter drank of the Spirit of God, everything changed. He was weak and he became strong, because the Bible says when we are weak, He is made strong.

...His faithfulness

Acts 5:15 so that they brought the sick out into the streets and laid them on beds and couches, that at least the shadow of Peter passing by might fall on some of them.

Acts 9:32 Now it came to pass, as Peter went through all *parts of the country,* that he also came down to the saints who dwelt in Lydda.

Acts 9:34 And Peter said to him, "Aeneas, Jesus the Christ heals you. Arise and make your bed." Then he arose immediately.

Acts 10:44-46 [44] While Peter was still speaking these words, the Holy Spirit fell upon all those who heard the word. [45] And those of the circumcision who believed were astonished, as many as came with Peter, because the gift of the Holy Spirit had been poured out on the Gentiles also. [46] For they heard them speak with tongues and magnify God.

We see all the work that Peter has done; it came to the point that the Lord used him more powerfully than he did all the other disciples. All the promises to him happened. Peter made promises to the Lord, but those promises failed. God made promises to Peter and they all came to pass. The first promise was for him to become a fisher of men and it was fulfilled when thousands of people came to Christ through his ministry. Second, was when the Lord promised him that he was going to build his church upon the rock, that rock was Peter's revelation of Christ. The second promise was fulfilled when all the people started to magnify God. When the people started to bring the sick people to the road and Peter's shadow would pass by and heal the sick. It is true that when we receive Christ into our lives and when we are baptized in the Holy Spirit we become more in God's likeness. We become more like Christ.

God does not concentrate on our failures, He focuses on His plan and destiny for us. My message is even though you have failed in your walk with Christ do not give up. As long as you are still breathing, you have hope. Your destiny is waiting for you. God's promise to you will never fail. Even though your promises to God have failed, His promises will always be faithful to you. The journey in life that I have been walking, there have been failures but I thank God that his promises have been faithful. All the prophesies that have been spoken over my life have come to pass and some are still coming. I hope for them in faith to come to pass. They will happen.

Chapter 10

Whom Does God Use?

The Son of a Witchdoctor

I was raised by witchdoctors and am the first to become a Christian in all the generations of my family. I grew up never knowing that one day God could use me. I heard His voice, while I was still a sinner; He talked to me before I gave my life to him. He showed me His love before I received him. I became His before I knew Him. I became His child, while my family was still taking control of my life. God's love is beyond measure. So today, not looking behind me, I am pressing forward to what God has for me. Now I am an overseer of thousands of churches, accompanied by signs and wonders. I became a pure vessel, and God is using this vessel, to carry his love, life, truth, joy and peace to all the people. Without a doubt, He started a work in me and He will finish it. His work is excellent. He desires all of us to operate the same way.

A Samaritan woman at the well

The Bible tells the story of a Samaritan woman at a well. Her life was a mess. She had no future, and she faced a daily reality of pain. She had no expectation that the Lord could use her life. She knew of no plan or strategy for her life.

She had no popularity or attraction to people around her… but instantly God used her life to change a city. What she had to do was just receive the Word. She became a doer of the word. Indeed, the whole city obeyed her and followed Jesus.

He is still seeking whom he can use

God is looking everywhere for one who can stand in the gap. He is not looking for the most intellectual, most educated, oldest, or youngest, he is looking for those who are obedient. This obedience is a death to self and a radical submission to His word.

I want to share the story of the frogs in Egypt. Frogs had been released all over the Egyptian Kingdom. Pharaoh called Moses and Aaron to pray for them to stop! Moses asked Pharaoh when he wanted the prayer and Pharaoh told him "tomorrow." Pharaoh postponed the prayer that was to be instant, while the people were in pain from the frogs. They needed immediate help, but he said "tomorrow". Tomorrow is not ours. Today is ours. Today, when you hear his word, do not hide it in your heart, receive it and live. Do not put off for tomorrow what you can do today. God calls us to live in "today!" His desire is that "today" will be the day of salvation, healing, deliverance, and walking with Him. Don't wait for tomorrow. Enter His Promises Today!

Exodus 8:8-10 [8] Then Pharaoh called for Moses and Aaron, and said, "Entreat the LORD that He may take away the frogs from me and from my people; and I will let the people go, that they may sacrifice to the LORD." [9] And Moses said to Pharaoh, "Accept the honor of saying when I shall intercede for you, for your servants, and for your people, to destroy the frogs from you and your houses, *that* they may remain in the river only." ¹⁰ So he said, "Tomorrow." And he said, "*Let it be* according to your word, that you may know that *there is* no one like the LORD our God.

Chapter 11

Going Back to the Holy Land

Song of Solomon 3:2-3
[2]" I will rise now," I said, And go about the city;
In the streets and in the squares
I will seek the one I love."
I sought him, but I did not find him.
[3] The watchmen who go about the city found me;
I said, "Have you seen the one I love?"

One day while in the Holy Land, I was looking out over the city that Jesus calls His. He appeared to me and He asked, "Did you see the One that I love?" I said, "Yes, I was on the tower of the Three Arches Hotel watching over the city." Again I said "Yes! This is the One that You love. You have chosen her for a time. You came for her but she was found by the watchman." He commissioned the watchman and the watchman received the commission to bring the one that He loves.

Then He said, "Tell her how much I love her. Tell her how much I long for her. Tell her how much I long to gather her. I need to protect her. I need to give her peace. Tell her how much I have been longing for her to be close to me. She is the only one that I love. I am coming to fetch her."

John 10:16 And other sheep I have which are not of this fold; them also I must bring, and they will hear My voice; and there will be one flock *and* one shepherd.

Jesus was talking about the Gentiles that were rushing into the Kingdom, and they became one flock in Abraham's house with one Shepherd, which is the true Messiah, the Son of God

John 10:27-28 [27]My sheep hear My voice, and I know them, and they follow Me. [28] And I give them eternal life, and they shall never perish; neither shall anyone snatch them out of My hand.

At the end of my tour across the land of Israel, I came to Jerusalem, to the feast of Tabernacles. When I arrived there, I walked all around Jerusalem and visited the children. I noticed that there was no peace and joy on their faces. The rumors of war had taken that away! I began to pray and ask God about the people. While I was praying, I heard the cry of Father Abraham. His cry was a longing to bring together the two sticks (the Jew and the Gentile) from his hand into oneness with him. While I was hearing this, I was standing on the tower at Three Arches Hotel. I looked down on the streets of Jerusalem and while I was looking, the picture changed immediately and I saw the people like dry bones. I saw them as a people longing for hope while Hope was within reach, looking for life while Life was within reach. Desiring a radical change, with tears on my face, I began to prophesy over the land. I said 'Live Again.'

The Lord asked a question to Ezekiel, "Can these dry bones live? Ezekiel answered, "Lord you know." The Lord knows the future of the Holy Land. The Lord said to Ezekiel, "Prophesy to these dry bones."

Ezekiel 37:3-6   ³ And He said to me, "Son of man, can these bones live?" So I answered, "O Lord GOD, You know." ⁴ Again He said to me, "Prophesy to these bones, and say to them, 'O dry bones, hear the word of the LORD! ⁵ Thus says the Lord GOD to these bones: "Surely I will cause breath to enter into you, and you shall live. ⁶ I will put sinews on you and bring flesh upon you, cover you with skin and put breath in you; and you shall live. Then you shall know that I *am* the LORD."'"

The Lord knew everything that was happening in the valley of the dry bones. He wanted Ezekiel to feel the love of the Father. He wanted Ezekiel to see that even though the bones were dry and hopeless, He was able to give hope. He needed to show Ezekiel how much He loved His people. The Lord had the power to give the dry bones life without the help of Ezekiel, but He wanted man to take part in the re-creation.

He needed the man to prophesy. I need you to command life to come to these dry bones. First, for me to give them bread, they have to hear the word of the Lord. If they hear the word of the Lord first, then I will cause my breath to enter into them. If they hear My Word, I will put sinews into them. If they hear My Word, I will put flesh on them, cover them with skin, and put My Breath into them. Then they will live forever.

My trip to Israel was a life-changing trip. The way we experienced the love of the Father was tremendous. There were 37 people in our group. We were unique in love. Our prayers for the Holy Land and for the land of Hebron were that none of his children should remain behind by not entering into his love. I believe there is coming a day of gathering to tie together the stick. It will be a day of so much joy and prosperity in the land of Hebron. First, hear the word of the Lord!

Matthew 23:37 "Jerusalem, Jerusalem, who kills the prophets and stones those who are sent to her! How often I wanted to gather your children together, the way a hen gathers her chicks under her wings, and you were unwilling."

Deuteronomy 32:11
Like an eagle that stirs up its nest,
That hovers over its young,
He spread His wings and caught them,
He carried them on His pinions. (NASB)

I have been asking God to reveal proofs about the Yeshua (Jesus) for twelve years. I started with far fewer evidences, or proofs, than I have now! I have prayed for people to be raised from the dead and have seen that happen. I have had many heavenly visions. But the evidence of Yeshua is far more than that. It really comes together when we get to the point that Jesus is really the Son of God. I saw evidences of Him when I was in Jerusalem. The Bible became so real. I saw the children come together in one house. The children of Ishmael and the children of Isaac came to offer their praise in one house. Though they came in from different directions, they came into one house. In the land of Israel, there is so much evidence of Yeshua. There is no escape from hearing about Him. Most of the people that we talked to, a majority from different beliefs, described a dream or vision of Him. God's heart from the beginning of time, and His plans, have all come together in Yeshua! He loves gathering His people together again.

> 2 Chronicles 36:15 And the LORD God of their fathers sent *warnings* to them by His messengers, rising up early and sending *them*, because He had compassion on His people and on His dwelling place.

As we were on the land, we felt the Spirit of the Father. In His mercy we could feel how He longed to gather His chicks in unity. We must understand and come to the place where we know that He longs for unity in His land and not division. He wants forgiveness on His land not anger. He wants peace and joy in His land. He wants obedience on His land. To the uttermost part of the world, we have to hear the word of the Lord and the Lord is one.

When we were in Israel, in a prayer room, I saw a light. It was neither the light of the sun nor the light of the moon but a light of the Spirit of the Lord.

> Joel 2:28 "And it shall come to pass afterward
> That I will pour out My Spirit on all flesh;
> Your sons and your daughters shall prophesy,
> Your old men shall dream dreams,
> Your young men shall see visions.

> Joel 2:32 And it shall come to pass *that* whoever calls on the name of the LORD shall be saved.

For in Mount Zion and in Jerusalem there shall be
deliverance, as the LORD has said,
Among the remnant whom the LORD calls.

Acts 2:1-4 [1] When the Day of Pentecost had fully come,
they were all with one accord in one place. [2]And suddenly
there came a sound from heaven, as of a rushing mighty
wind, and it filled the whole house where they were sitting.
[3]Then there appeared to them divided tongues, as of fire,
and one sat upon each of them. [4]And they were all filled
with the Holy Spirit and began to speak with other
tongues, as the Spirit gave them utterance.

Acts 2:21 And it shall come to pass that whoever calls on
the name of the LORD shall be saved.'

That light was revelation of the fulfillment of the book
of Joel in the book of Acts. This to us, who believe in Christ, is
our assurance because many people have the question, how can
I know that I am really a child of God. They say, "How can I
have assurance of my salvation." Especially to the children of
Israel, they now have so much doubt, that doubt gives them a
fear of serving Yeshua because they think that they will be
serving other God's. To some of them, even though they are
having visions and dreams, they are waiting for something.
They are waiting for more evidence, more proof of Yeshua.
They want evidence to be clearer than it already is.

The evidence has already come openly and clearly. I
received a few answers to those questions because all the
Christians know that they are sinners and cannot save
themselves. They are in need of a Savior, the Savior has come,
and that is why they have assurance of where they are going
after this life. Secondly, they know by the love they have for

one another and thirdly, they know by the freedom they have in serving God. These are the assurances that Christians have.

On the Sea of Galilee as we had been praying and seeking the face of the Lord, the Lord touched our lives in new ways; we were filled with the Spirit of God and filled with joy. Many tourists came from different nations and they joined us in oneness. We began to call upon the name of the Lord declaring life and harmony again upon the land to the children of Ishmael and Isaac!

The Cities of Refuge

Numbers 35:13-14 [13]And of the cities which you give, you shall have six cities of refuge. [14] You shall appoint three cities on this side of the Jordan, and three cities you shall appoint in the land of Canaan, *which* will be cities of refuge.

God commanded Moses to build the cities of refuge so that when someone broke the law he could run to them to escape for their life. These cities were built on both sides of the Jordan River, three to the west and three to the east of the Jordan River. The Jordan represented death. God told the Israelites to live and focus on him. Those cities represented the Trinity, whether you believe it or not God is one, Father, Son and Holy Spirit they are one. While we are still on earth, we live with the Father, Son and Holy Spirit. When we cross the river of 'death' we will also live by the Father, Son and Holy Spirit. They are our refuge in this life and the life to come. Even though Moses did not cross over to the other side of the Jordan, he went to Mount Nebo and he did not come back. That is where he crosses the river of death and he goes to live with the Trinity of God, so that the word can be fulfilled. For the Word says 'for in him we live and move and have our being...' Acts 17:28a.

> Isaiah 55:3 Incline your ear and come to Me.
> Listen, that you may live; And I will make an everlasting covenant with you, According to the faithful mercies shown to David. (NASB)

Chapter 12

Abiding In Jesus

The Anointing

One of the promised characteristics of the last days anointing is that the Holy Spirit will lead and instruct us through dreams, visions, and revelations of the Lord. That is our promise and our privilege as the Spirit of the Lord instructs us in the ways of the Kingdom.

The Scriptures declare:

> Psalms 16:7 I will bless the LORD who has given me counsel; My heart also instructs me in the night seasons.

1 John 2:20,27-28 ²⁰ But you have an anointing from the Holy One, and you know all things. ²⁷ But the anointing which you have received from Him abides in you, and you do not need that anyone teach you; but as the same anointing teaches you concerning all things, and is true, and is not a lie, and just as it has taught you, you will abide in Him. ²⁸ And now, little children, abide in Him, that when He appears, we may have confidence and not be ashamed before Him at His coming.

The Scriptures say, the anointing will teach you. Anointing is so important. David, reveals the power of anointing on his life. It wasn't simple strength that gave him the ability to kill the bear and the lion. It wasn't simply strength that killed the giant. When the anointing is with us, we will have the strategy and plan of how to defeat demonic activities. We need God's anointing to be our protection just like David. Even though he was fighting with the lion, the lion could not defeat him because he was anointed. We need God's anointing, for fighting against evil spirits, disease and sickness, just as David before the giant. Even though the giant was coming to David with all his weapons, Goliath could not defeat the anointed one. God's anointing is for our protection and power, teaching as the scriptures say, to give us strategy and most of all to reveal the heart of the Father.

We cannot receive God's anointing by obeying the law. David was not anointed because of the law. It does not come because you are very intellectual -- David was not intellectual. It comes because of obedience. You can be anointed many times. David was first anointed as a shepherd boy and I believe that anointing helped him to tend the sheep. One thing that I learned from David's anointing, is that after he became anointed he remained faithful to his father's sheep. We have to learn to be faithful with the little, and after he was faithful with the sheep, God granted David to be king over Israel. He was anointed the second time.

The Lord oftentimes chooses the night seasons to release His counsel and instruction along with divine strategy for the season in which we are living. With these important insights, we can more readily prepare ourselves and sow diligently into the anointing, that we might reap an abundant harvest of Kingdom fruit.

Get Understanding

Psalms 119:27 Make me understand the way of Your precepts; So shall I meditate on Your wonderful works.

Psalms 119:144 The righteousness of your testimonies *is* everlasting; Give me understanding, and I shall live.

The plea of David in Psalm 119, the same prayer that he prayed repeatedly, was to have God's understanding. There is so much that we need to understand. Whenever I read Psalm 119, I think of this man -- he was a king, he had all the counselors and mighty men and soldiers with him, yet still he knew there was something he needed to understand. That is why he continued to request the same thing repetitively in the same chapter. That is why Apostle Paul prayed this prayer in Ephesians.

Ephesians 1:18 the eyes of your understanding being enlightened; that you may know what is the hope of His calling, what are the riches of the glory of His inheritance in the saints,

Psalms 119:169 Let my cry come before You, O LORD; Give me understanding according to Your word.

Philippians 2:3-4 ³Do nothing from selfishness or empty conceit, but with humility of mind regard one another as more important than yourselves; ⁴do not merely look out for your own personal interests, but also for the interests of others. (NASB)

This is where I see true Christian understanding; it is opposite of what the world thinks. So much selfishness and ambition leads to people being proud and ignorant of God. Really, no one can say to himself 'I am the most humble person on earth,' -- the fruits of humility speak for themselves. Pray for the fruits of humility to be visible in your life. That passage in Philippians reveals the true fruits of humility.

Amos 3:7 declares: "Surely the Lord GOD does nothing Unless He reveals His secret counsel to His servants the prophets." (NASB)

Revelation 1:1 The Revelation of Jesus Christ, which God gave Him to show His servants—things which must shortly take place. And He sent and signified *it* by His angel to His servant John,

The Profit of Abiding in Jesus

Jesus warned us about the false prophet. False prophets and false teachers are coming and he told us how we are going to see them when they come. You will know them by their fruits so if you want to know about whether or not they are true or false prophets, examine the fruit with Galatians 5 as the plumbline.

Galatians 5:22-23 But the fruit of the Spirit is love, joy, peace, longsuffering, kindness, goodness, faithfulness, gentleness, self-control. Against such there is no law.

When any teacher comes in the name of the Lord saying that he is a teacher, prophet or apostle, we as believers are encouraged to check the fruit of their ministry. We must judge fruit to see where it comes from. If you are a preacher don't go out without fruit. Don't go out preaching without fruit, first you have to bear fruit and then take the fruit to the people. You cannot bear fruit if you are not abiding in Jesus and keeping His Word. You will then receive the promise of the Holy Spirit and the Holy Spirit is the giver of the fruits. With fruit, you are free to go. With fruit, you can share with your brothers. With fruit, the people will see you as a true prophet, apostle or teacher because they will see the fruit in you.

> **You cannot bear fruit if you are not abiding in Jesus and keeping His Word.**

Matthew 24:11 Then many false prophets will rise up and deceive many.

Matthew 7:15-16 "Beware of false prophets, who come to you in sheep's clothing, but inwardly they are ravenous wolves. You will know them by their fruits. Do men gather grapes from thornbushes or figs from thistles?

Mark 13:22 For false christs and false prophets will rise and show signs and wonders to deceive, if possible, even the elect.

The Bible says false prophets will perform great miracles that will mislead the people. In the Old Testament, Moses' rod became a snake; the sorcerers came and turned their rods into snakes as well. Great signs and miracles are not always God. It seems as if the whole world is being convinced of the supernatural. Because of the influence of the media, many people are aware of magical things. Jesus is not something magical. Jesus is real. A long time before the influence of the media, across the continent of Africa, most people were living in the care of witchdoctors. The witchdoctors taught the people about the supernatural. They know we live in both worlds, the physical and spiritual. The majority of the people in Africa know the spiritual world to a great degree. When someone comes to Christ, they see the difference between the spiritual world of the witchdoctor and the real one. Even though we live with both of these types of worlds around us, we as Christians are called to bear fruit. As the Bible says, even though we live in this world we are not of this world.

2 Peter 2:1-2 But there were also false prophets among the people, even as there will be false teachers among you, who will secretly bring in destructive heresies, even denying the Lord who bought them, *and* bring on themselves swift destruction. And many will follow their destructive ways, because of whom the way of truth will be blasphemed.

The Bible is true in saying the way of truth is spoken of as evil because of the false prophets and teachers. This started because of believers that do not abide in the Word. If we do not abide in the Word, soon the fruit will start falling off of us and go bad and the fruit of the evil one will start growing. My encouragement to you is to stay focused on the Word of Jesus

Christ, stay close to God all the time, pray without ceasing that your fruit may remain – and that your heart may remain true and faithful to Jesus too!

Matthew 7:16 You shall know them by their fruits.

Revelation 19:20 and the beast was taken, and with him the false prophet who did the signs before him, in which he led astray those who did receive the mark of the beast, and those who did bow before his image; living they were cast -- the two -- to the lake of the fire, that is burning with brimstone; (YLT)

Revelation 20:10 and the Devil, who is leading them astray, was cast into the lake of fire and brimstone, where [are] the beast and the false prophet, and they shall be tormented day and night -- to the ages of the ages. (YLT)

False prophets come from the evil one. They are supporters of the beast and the beast with them and with all those who follow the beast. Those who did not want to bear the fruit and who did not remain faithful in the ministry of the Word. They have been drinking the wine of his lies. The final end for them is the lake of fire. So come out of him, sink into the Word, bear fruit, and pray that your fruit may not fall off your life but rather that you will bear much fruit because you abide in Him

John 15:4-8 [4] Abide in Me, and I in you. As the branch cannot bear fruit of itself, unless it abides in the vine, neither can you, unless you abide in Me. [5] "I am the vine, you *are* the branches. He who abides in Me, and I in him, bears much fruit; for without Me you can do nothing. [6] If anyone does not abide in Me, he is cast out as a branch and is withered; and they gather them and throw *them* into the fire, and they are burned. [7] If you abide in Me, and My words abide in you, you will ask what you desire, and it shall be done for you. [8] By this My Father is glorified, that you bear much fruit; so you will be My disciples.

The world will see our fruit because we will have fruit when we abide in him all the time in prayer, fellowship, in reading the Word and having intimate time with Jesus. The fruit of the Holy Spirit is for us to support His ministry through our lives. We have to make sure that we have the fruit in our lives and that the fruit is visible. They are not hidden fruit. If you have fruit, there will be testimony of others about your life. The evidence of fruit helps us know when we are on the right track. Some fruit you may know about, but other fruit must be revealed to others as they see it working in you!.

We will have a revelation and knowledge of him as we seek his face. Again, we will need the help of the Holy Spirit to guide us, protect us, and teach us as we are abiding in Him. My recommendation to my dear reader is to stay in the Word, pray in the Holy Spirit all the time, bear fruit, pray for the protection of your fruits to remain fresh in your life. AMEN

How do we abide in Him? Spend time in intimacy with him in prayer. The Holy Spirit may only reveal the wisdom hidden in Him.

John 7:15-17 ^{15} The Jews then were astonished, saying, "How has this man become learned, having never been educated?" ^{16} So Jesus answered them and said, "My teaching is not Mine, but His who sent Me. ^{17} "If anyone is willing to do His will, he will know of the teaching, whether it is of God or whether I speak from Myself. (NASB)

Acts 4:13 Now as they observed the confidence of Peter and John and understood that they were uneducated and untrained men, they were amazed, and began to recognize them as having been with Jesus. (NASB)

Acts 4:31 And when they had prayed, the place where they had gathered together was shaken, and they were all filled with the Holy Spirit and began to speak the word of God with boldness. (NASB)

Ephesians 2:5-6 ^{5}even when we were dead in our transgressions, made us alive together with Christ (by grace you have been saved), ^{6} and raised us up with Him, and seated us with Him in the heavenly places in Christ Jesus, (NASB)

1 Corinthians 2:4-11 [4] and my message and my preaching were not in persuasive words of wisdom, but in demonstration of the Spirit and of power, [5] so that your faith would not rest on the wisdom of men, but on the power of God. [6] Yet we do speak wisdom among those who are mature; a wisdom, however, not of this age nor of the rulers of this age, who are passing away; [7] but we speak God's wisdom in a mystery, the hidden wisdom which God predestined before the ages to our glory; [8] the wisdom which none of the rulers of this age has understood; for if they had understood it they would not have crucified the Lord of glory; [9] but just as it is written,
"Things which eye has not seen
    and ear has not heard,
And which have not entered the heart of man,
    All that God has prepared for those who love Him."
[10] For to us God revealed them through the Spirit; for the Spirit searches all things, even the depths of God.
[11] For who among men knows the thoughts of a man except the spirit of the man which is in him? Even so the thoughts of God no one knows except the Spirit of God. (NASB)

He was Brought Forth for Us

He was there to cover our Nakedness

When the Israelites came out of Egypt they were celebrating, singing and dancing after the crossing of the red sea. The famine came; they were thirsty and had very minimal possessions. The Hebrews began to cry and complain, so the Lord began to feed them with their hearts desire. He overwhelmed them with their hearts desire! When it was too much on them, they started to rebel against God and his servant Moses but God' grace never departed from his people.

When there was no water, he gave them drink. When there was no food, he gave them food to eat. When they faced the battle of the snakes, he provided the snake that gave life when it was looked upon; and they were given life for free. It was hard for them to be obedient all the time and God gave them the Law. It was their statement of faith in order to serve God easily. It gave them daily statutes to help them personally and throughout the whole congregation of Israel.

Eventually, they became rebellious to the Law that the Lord gave to them as a chosen generation and a royal priesthood in God's house.

It was not good in God's eyes when he saw people being stoned for breaking the Law. He began to reveal his grace and God's grace was never to depart from his people.

Proverbs 8:24-32

24 When there were no depths I was brought forth,
When there were no springs abounding with water.
25 Before the mountains were settled,
Before the hills I was brought forth;
26 While He had not yet made the earth and the fields,
Nor the first dust of the world.
27 When He established the heavens, I was there,
When He inscribed a circle on the face of the deep,
28 When He made firm the skies above,
When the springs of the deep became fixed,
29 When He set for the sea its boundary
So that the water would not transgress His command,
When He marked out the foundations of the earth;

³⁰ Then I was beside Him, as a master workman;
And I was daily His delight,
Rejoicing always before Him,
³¹ Rejoicing in the world, His earth,
And having my delight in the sons of men.
³² Now therefore, O sons, listen to me,
For blessed are they who keep my ways. (NASB)

Isaiah 14:11-17
¹¹ Your pomp is brought down to Sheol,
And the sound of your stringed instruments;
The maggot is spread under you,
And worms cover you.
¹² How you are fallen from heaven,
O Lucifer, son of the morning!
How you are cut down to the ground,
You who weakened the nations!
¹³ For you have said in your heart:
' I will ascend into heaven,
I will exalt my throne above the stars of God;
I will also sit on the mount of the congregation
On the farthest sides of the north;
¹⁴ I will ascend above the heights of the clouds,
I will be like the Most High.'
¹⁵ Yet you shall be brought down to Sheol,
To the lowest depths of the Pit.
¹⁶ " Those who see you will gaze at you,
And consider you, saying:
'Is this the man who made the earth tremble,
Who shook kingdoms
¹⁷ Who made the world as a wilderness
And destroyed its cities,
Who did not open the house of his prisoners?'

Revelation 12:7-9
[7] And there was war in heaven, Michael and his angels waging war with the dragon The dragon and his angels waged war,
[8] and they were not strong enough, and there was no longer a place found for them in heaven.
[9] And the great dragon was thrown down, the serpent of old who is called the devil and Satan, who deceives the whole world; he was thrown down to the earth, and his angels were thrown down with him. (NASB)

Genesis 2:7-9 [7] And the LORD God formed man *of* the dust of the ground, and breathed into his nostrils the breath of life; and man became a living being. [8] The LORD God planted a garden eastward in Eden, and there He put the man whom He had formed. [9] And out of the ground the LORD God made every tree grow that is pleasant to the sight and good for food. The tree of life *was* also in the midst of the garden, and the tree of the knowledge of good and evil.

Luke 10:18-19 [18] And He said to them, "I saw Satan fall like lightning from heaven. [19] Behold, I give you the authority to trample on serpents and scorpions, and over all the power of the enemy, and nothing shall by any means hurt you.

Genesis 3:21 The LORD God made garments of skin for Adam and his wife, and clothed them. (NASB)

When sacrifices were made, the animal that was killed represented Jesus. He is only one that can cover our nakedness and shame in life.

Genesis 3:22 Then the LORD God said, "Behold, the man has become like one of Us, knowing good and evil; and now, he might stretch out his hand, and take also from the tree of life, and eat, and live forever"--(NASB)

> **Now God's desire is that we have to be like Him even more and more and that's why He gave us His Son, even most of all His Holy Spirit**

...and that tree is Jesus and that tree was kept for you and me.

He was there as a Lamb for Sacrifice

Genesis 22:7-13
[7] Isaac spoke to Abraham his father and said, "My father!" And he said, "Here I am, my son." And he said, "Behold, the fire and the wood, but where is the lamb for the burnt offering?"
[8] Abraham said, "God will provide for Himself the lamb for the burnt offering, my son." So the two of them walked on together.
[9] Then they came to the place of which God had told him; and Abraham built the altar there and arranged the wood, and bound his son Isaac and laid him on the altar, on top of the wood.
[10] Abraham stretched out his hand and took the knife to slay his son.
[11] But the angel of the LORD called to him from heaven and said, "Abraham, Abraham!" And he said, "Here I am."

[12] He said, "Do not stretch out your hand against the lad, and do nothing to him; for now I know that you fear God, since you have not withheld your son, your only son, from Me."
[13] Then Abraham raised his eyes and looked, and behold, behind him a ram caught in the thicket by his horns; and Abraham went and took the ram and offered him up for a burnt offering in the place of his son. (NASB)

Exodus 12:46 It is to be eaten in a single house; you are not to bring forth any of the flesh outside of the house, nor are you to break any bone of it. (NASB)

He took the place of Isaac on Mount Moriah. Finally, he took our place of sin and death that we can become GOD's children, pure and with eternal life.

John 1:29 The next day John saw Jesus coming toward him and said, "Look! The Lamb of God who takes away the sin of the world!" (NLT)

He was the Way in the Red Sea

Exodus 14:21-22 (NASB)
[21] Then Moses stretched out his hand over the sea; and the LORD swept the sea back by a strong east wind all night and turned the sea into dry land, so the waters were divided. [22] The sons of Israel went through the midst of the sea on the dry land, and the waters were like a wall to them on their right hand and on their left.

He became a Way to the place that seemed impossible. He is still the Way to our needs and difficulties in life.

John 14:6 Jesus said to him, "I am the way, and the truth, and the life; no one comes to the Father but through Me." (NASB)

He was there as a healing tree

Exodus 15:23-25 [23] When they came to Marah, they could not drink the waters of Marah, for they were bitter; therefore it was named Marah. [24] So the people grumbled at Moses, saying, "What shall we drink?" [25]Then he cried out to the LORD, and the LORD showed him a tree; and he threw it into the waters, and the waters became sweet There He made for them a statute and regulation, and there He tested them. (NASB)

And that tree is Jesus

John 15:1-5 [1] I am the True Vine, and My Father is the Vinedresser. [2] Every branch in Me that does not bear fruit, He takes away. And every one that bears fruit, He prunes it so that it may bring forth more fruit. [3] You are already clean because of the word which I have spoken to you. [4] Abide in Me, and I in you. As the branch cannot bear fruit of itself unless it abides in the vine, so neither can you unless you abide in Me. [5] I am the vine, you are the branches; he who abides in Me and I in him, he bears much fruit, for apart from Me you can do nothing. (NASB)

He was there as a bread to them

Exodus 16:11-12 [11] And the LORD spoke to Moses, saying, [12] I have heard the grumblings of the sons of Israel; speak to them, saying, 'At twilight you shall eat meat, and in the morning you shall be filled with bread; and you shall know that I am the LORD your God.' (NASB)

John 6: 47-51 [47]"Truly, truly, I say to you, he who believes has eternal life. [48] I am the bread of life. [49] Your fathers ate the manna in the wilderness, and they died. [50] This is the bread which comes down out of heaven, so that one may eat of it and not die. [51] I am the living bread that came down out of heaven; if anyone eats of this bread, he will live forever; and the bread also which I will give for the life of the world is My flesh." (NASB)

He is the Rock

Exodus 17:5-6 [5]And the LORD said to Moses, "Go on before the people, and take with you some of the elders of Israel. Also take in your hand your rod with which you struck the river, and go. [6] Behold, I will stand before you there on the rock in Horeb; and you shall strike the rock, and water will come out of it, that the people may drink." And Moses did so in the sight of the elders of Israel.

1 Corinthians 10:3-4 all ate the same spiritual food, and all drank the same spiritual drink. For they drank of that spiritual Rock that followed them, and that Rock was Christ

Numbers 20:8 "Take the rod; you and your brother Aaron gather the congregation together. Speak to the rock before their eyes, and it will yield its water; thus you shall bring water for them out of the rock, and give drink to the congregation and their animals."

...and that Rock was Christ

Deuteronomy 32:4 *He is* the Rock;
   His work *is* perfect.
   For all His ways *are* justice,

A God of truth and without injustice;
Righteous and upright *is* He.

Deuteronomy 32:13
   "He made him ride in the heights of the earth,
   That he might eat the produce of the fields;
   He made him draw honey from the rock,
   And oil from the flinty rock;

...and that Rock was Christ

Deuteronomy 32:18 You deserted the Rock, who fathered
you; you forgot the God who gave you birth. (NIV)

...and that Rock was Christ

Judges 13:19 Then Manoah took a young goat, together
with the grain offering, and sacrificed it on a rock to the
LORD. And the LORD did an amazing thing while Manoah
and his wife watched: (NIV)

...and that Rock was Christ

I Samuel 2:2
   "There is no one holy like the LORD;
   there is no one besides you;
   there is no Rock like our God. (NIV)

...and that Rock was Christ

II Samuel 22:3 my God is my rock, in whom I take refuge,
my shield and the horn of my salvation.
He is my stronghold, my refuge and my savior—
from violent men you save me. (NIV)

...and that Rock was Christ

II Samuel 22:47
   "The LORD lives! Praise be to my Rock!
   Exalted be God, the Rock, my Savior! (NIV)

...and that Rock was Christ

Job 29:6 when I washed my steps with curds,
and the rock poured out rivers of oil for me; (NIV)

...and that Rock was Christ

Psalms 18:46 The LORD lives! Praise be to my Rock!
Exalted be God my Savior! (NIV)

...and that Rock was Christ

Psalms 31:3 For You are my rock and my fortress;
   Therefore, for Your name's sake,
   Lead me and guide me.

...and that Rock was Christ

Psalms 62:7 In God *is* my salvation and my glory;
   The rock of my strength,
   And my refuge, *is* in God.

...and that Rock was Christ

Psalms 78:35 Then they remembered that God *was* their
rock, And the Most High God their Redeemer.

...and that Rock was Christ

Isaiah 2:10 Enter into the rock, and hide in the dust,
   From the terror of the LORD
   And the glory of His majesty.

...and that Rock was Christ

Isaiah 51:1 "Listen to Me, you who follow after righteousness, You who seek the LORD: Look to the rock *from which* you were hewn, And to the hole of the pit *from which* you were dug.

...and that Rock was Christ

Matthew 7:24 "Therefore whoever hears these sayings of Mine, and does them, I will liken him to a wise man who built his house on the rock:

...and that Rock was Christ

I Corinthians 10:4 and all drank the same spiritual drink. For they drank of that spiritual Rock that followed them, and that Rock was Christ.

Because of This Rock that is in us. Because we have the joy of following Him into the world. Because our eyes are being opened to see what He sees... that it's harvest time!

What are you waiting for? The Harvest is waiting for you! It's Rush Hour!